Moses said: "Show me your glory, I pray." And God said, "I will make all my goodness pass before you. . . . But . . . you can not see my face; for no one shall see me and live." And the Lord continued, "See there is a place by me where you shall stand on the rock; and while my glory passes by I will put you in the cleft of the rock, and I will cover you with my hand until I have passed by; then I will take away my hand, and you shall see my back; but my face shall not be seen."

EXODUS 33:18-23

In you O Lord, I seek refuge;
  do not let me ever be put to shame;
  in your righteousness deliver me.
Incline your ear to me;
  rescue me speedily.
Be a rock of refuge for me,
  a strong fortress to save me.

PS. 31:1-2

When we cry "Abba! Father," it is that very Spirit bearing witness with our spirit that we are children of God, and if children, then heirs, heirs of God and joint heirs with Christ — if in fact we suffer with him so that we may also be glorified with him.

ROMANS 8:15-17

THE SHADOW
OF THE ALMIGHTY

Father, Son, and Spirit in Biblical Perspective

Ben Witherington III

&

Laura M. Ice

WILLIAM B. EERDMANS PUBLISHING COMPANY

GRAND RAPIDS, MICHIGAN / CAMBRIDGE, U.K.

Wm. B. Eerdmans Publishing Co.
255 Jefferson Ave. S.E., Grand Rapids, Michigan 49503 /
P.O. Box 163, Cambridge CB3 9PU U.K.

Printed in the United States of America

07 06 05 04 03 02   7 6 5 4 3 2 1

Library of Congress Cataloging-in-Publication Data

Witherington, Ben, 1951-
The shadow of the Almighty: Father, Son, and Spirit in biblical perspective /
Ben Witherington III & Laura M. Ice.
p.   cm.
Includes bibliographical references.
ISBN 0-8028-3948-7 (pbk.: alk. paper)
1. Bible. N.T. — Theology.   2. Trinity — Biblical teaching.
I. Ice, Laura Michaels, 1964-   II. Title.

BS2398.W58   2002
225 — dc21

2001053855

www.eerdmans.com

To our precious families:
To Ann, Christy, David, and Julia
and to Jeffrey, Ian, and Danielle.

May the grace of the Lord Jesus Christ,
The love of God
And the fellowship of the Holy Spirit
Be our refuge, now and forever.

Contents

—❦—

Fore-words

—⦚—

M ention the term "theology" and different things come to mind for different people. For some the term may encompass the whole subject matter of the New Testament, or at least all the traditional standing topics usually discussed under this heading — the doctrine of God, the doctrine of salvation, the doctrine of eschatology, and even theological anthropology (e.g., Paul's anthropological terms). This study has the more modest goal of examining some, and only some, of the crucial God language in the New Testament, in particular the language about God being Father, Son, and Holy Spirit.

To some, such an exercise may seem either illegitimate or passé. It could be argued that there are only theologies in the New Testament, not a theology of the NT, and therefore it is inappropriate to talk about New Testament Theology writ large. On the other hand, there will be others who feel that they have had quite enough of the use of paternal language for God and that this study will be at best arcane and at worst a perpetuation of a theological problem. We do not feel that either of these criticisms is entirely valid, though each has a point to make.

Whether we agree with how the earliest Christians discoursed about God, or not, it can hardly be disputed that they did refer to God as Father, Son, and Holy Spirit. At the very least then, it is an appropriate historical undertaking to ask and try to answer the question of what they understood by using these terms. While it is true enough that different NT authors do have differing theological emphases, and sometimes differing terminology, all NT writers to one degree or another use the traditional language that came to be called Trinitarian language. This was indeed something that distinguished them from other groups that were part of or came forth from early Judaism. It is a fundamental assumption of this study that however much diversity there was in early Christianity, there was also some significant unity, particularly in the use of God language, and we would do well to examine closely these shared terms and the concepts they represent. Indeed, we would also do well to ask about the shared experiences of God that the earliest Christians had.

The modus operandi of this study will be to examine the traditional God language right across the NT canon and see what comes to light, which is to say this study will take a canonical approach to theology. This assumes that early Christianity was a relatively unified movement with a shared theological tradition. Care will be taken not to artificially blend together disparate ideas or traditions, but at the same time we will be looking for what the earliest Christians shared in common both in regard to the use and the function of their God language. For those of us for whom the canonical discourse is seen as normative in some sense, there will also surely be implications for modern faith and practice.

In regard to the modern concerns about inclusive language we must urge that while we fully support the use of such language when referring to human beings, we find unconvincing the arguments that "Father" language or "Son" language should no longer be used in the naming of God. It is of course true that abuses have happened in the use of such language throughout church history, as the church was all too captive to patriarchal agendas and did often oppress women and others by the way they used their God language. Yet the old Latin dictum remains true — "Abusus non tollit usum." The abuse of something does not rule out its proper use. Nor does the argument that we should not use Father language for God because there have often been abusive human fathers convince at the end of the day. Unless one is actually prepared to argue that there are no good fathers, or there have never been good models of what fatherhood should look like, it should not be seen as inappropriate (then or now) to use such language for God. Indeed, to eschew using such language altogether is to deliberately disobey Jesus' command that when we pray to God we should at least some of the time pray to God as *abba*, just as Jesus did himself.

A canonical approach to God language will indeed wish to affirm the proper use of the traditional God language while also emphasizing that other sorts of language, including female metaphors, exist in the canon when the functioning of God is being described. In short, a canonical approach will wish to embrace all such materials as valid and valuable when we are talking about a God who is spirit, and therefore in the divine essence is neither male nor female.

Nevertheless, a word of caution is in order. A Gnostic approach to the Son will not do, for he was in his human nature a man, and his human nature should not be radically separated from his divine nature. Theology that tries to bracket out or protect itself from the human nature of Jesus of Nazareth, or from Jesus as a historical person, is not truly Christian theology either insofar as it is consonant with the beliefs and practices of earliest Christians, or of the normal and normative beliefs and practices of the church today. Our task in this book is to re-examine that traditional language in the New Testament and see what indeed the earliest Christians believed about the nature and functions of the God they called Father, Son, and Holy Spirit. In this particular study we will limit our selves to these three terms and their occurrences in the NT.

Finally, it needs to be stressed that while it is quite true that there is no developed doctrine of the Trinity enunciated in the New Testament, there is nonetheless the raw data to construct such a doctrine. There is an especial wealth of material about the relationship of the Son to the Father, and of the Spirit to the Son. Furthermore, as we shall see, such God language was not as radical a departure from early Jewish monotheism as many have thought. We will be drawing on recent gains in the study of early Jewish thinking about monotheism by R. Bauckham and others to show how there was considerable continuity between Christologically reformulated monotheism and other forms of early Jewish monotheism.

Thus, this study will appear by turns both controversial in some quarters, and commonplace in others. So be it. Our concern must be to faithfully examine the details of the language about Father, Son, and Spirit as it is found in the New Testament and let the implications be drawn as the reader chooses. We invite the reader on a journey through the storied world of the New Testament as we seek to reflect on God and the divine roles in that story. We trust the journey will prove both stimulating and also reassuring, both convicting and convincing. It is time then to examine first of all the story of the "Promising" Father.

CHAPTER ONE

The Story Thus Far

—⟨ℯ⁄ℯ⟩—

The God of the Old Testament offered revelation to God's people in various forms and under various names and images. Whether we think of Elohim or Adonai or what appears to be the more personal name Yahweh, it is nonetheless striking that God is seldom named as or prayed to as Father in the Hebrew Scriptures. There are of course famous passages like Hos. 11:1ff., but even there the word *'abh* does not occur. The analogy is drawn between a good father's activities in his relationship to his son. The same sort of use of the language of analogy appears in Ps. 103:13 ("as a father has compassion on his children, so the Lord has compassion on those who fear him") or in Prov. 3:12 where we learn that God reproves the one God loves, as a father reproves a beloved son. We must then be able to distinguish between the use of paternal analogies and the naming of God as Father, especially because in the Ancient Near East (henceforth ANE) the name of a god connoted something real and vital about the nature of that God.

One possible case where God may be named as Father in the Pentateuch is Deut. 32:6 in the Song of Moses, where we hear "Is this the way you repay the Lord, O you foolish and unwise people? Is he not your Father who created you, who made you and established you?" The word "Father" in this verse could be capitalized. The reference suggests the relational nature of the language. One can't be a father unless one has one or more children. Thus when the subject is God as creator of human beings and in particular God's own people, the Father language quite naturally comes into play. Yet as W. Brueggemann stresses, the Father imagery does not likely suggest a biological begetting, here or elsewhere in the Hebrew Scriptures.[1]

This same sort of idea of father comes into play in Is. 45:9-11. A father is like a potter who has the right to shape his children and their actions as he wishes, without giving an account of these actions. So also Yahweh the creator of a people has the right to shape them as Yahweh sees fit. This example is interesting because it assumes God is fatherlike, but it draws an analogy with a potter's functions and prerogatives. Of a similar nature to this last example is the one reasonably clear exception in the OT to the rule of no address of God as Father, found in Is. 64:7(8): "You are our Father; we are the clay, and you are the potter."

Mal. 2:10 also makes the connection between being a father and creating: "Have we all not one father? Has not one God created us?" Here again the connection between creating people and the Father language is reasonably clear. Yet ominously, Mal. 1:6 affirms that Israel does not honor and fear its divine Father.

We may also wish to point to several prophetic texts as possible exceptions to the rule about naming God as Father in the OT. In Jer. 3:19 God's people are upbraided with the words: "I thought you would call me, my Father, and would not turn from following me." The implication is that God's people have *not* addressed God in this way, though it was something God had hoped for. Notice too here the connection with the estrangement from God. Instead of having an intimate relationship with God characterized in familial terms, just the opposite was happening. Israel was turning away from God and ceasing to follow God's ways. Jer. 31:9 also emphasized that it is God's own earnest desire to relate to his people as a father. He will protect those returning from exile "for I am a father to Israel, and Ephraim is my firstborn."

Finally, there are a few texts where God is said to have a special fa-

1. See W. Brueggemann, *Theology of the Old Testament* (Minneapolis: Fortress Press, 1997), pp. 244-47.

ther-son relationship with the king. For instance, we find this language in Ps. 2:7 in the coronation ode: "You are my son, today I have begotten you." The begetting language that is normally avoided when referring to God as Father is found here, but here the language is used purely metaphorically to speak about a sort of official adoption of the king such that he becomes in title and position God's son. It is the reference to begetting which makes clear that God is imaged as father here, since the word "father" is not mentioned in this text. Similarly we find the promise in the prophecy in 2 Sam. 7:14, "I will be his father, and he shall be my son." Once in Ps. 89:26-28 it is said the king will address Yahweh as "Father, God, and Rock of his salvation."[2]

Thus, having surveyed the few relevant references, we can only agree with Brueggemann that images such as Yahweh as judge, or Yahweh as warrior, or Yahweh as king, are far more prevalent in the Hebrew Scriptures. Yet when we do find the Father language it suggests God's compassion and care, God's creating and sustaining roles in relationship to Israel, or God's official adopting of the king as his son.[3] The father "image for Yahweh provides a way in which Israel can speak about Yahweh's profound commitment to Israel, a commitment on which Israel can count for special, positive attention." However, it "is evident that the father, while tender and generous, is not romantic about the relationship but is capable of regret and fierceness. In Jer. 3:19 and 31:9 and Hos. 11:1-9 the metaphor of father is employed in order to

2. On the above discussion see H. Ringgren, "'abh," *Theological Dictionary of the Old Testament*, vol. 1, pp. 16-19.

3. In the categorization offered by M. Meye Thompson, *The Promise of the Father* (Louisville: Westminster/John Knox, 2000), p. 39: (1) God is father in the sense of the origin of a family of people or the one who provides an inheritance to his children; (2) God is the father who provides for and protects his children; (3) obedience and honor are due to the father. The problem with this taxonomy is that it does indeed start within the functions of human fathers and then predicates them of God, assuming that the conceptions come from patriarchal culture in the first place. But no human father is seen as the origin of the universe or of all creation or of a whole people, and yet we have such associations of creator and father in the OT. Thompson is likely right, however, that the distinction between nature and qualities probably did not really exist in antiquity (p. 38). There is, however, a difference between naming and drawing analogies.

exhibit the tension between fierceness and compassion in the inclination of Yahweh. In these texts, as in Psalm 103, Yahweh's compassion prevails."[4] Yahweh then is Father in the sense that he makes Israel's life possible at all, being the creator, and in the sense that Yahweh has a close relationship with and concern for Israel once it exists as a people, especially with Israel's king. Note, however, that it seems to be only certain special individuals, like the king, that are singled out for a personal relationship with Yahweh, the Father.

To what do we attribute this general lack of addressing God as Father,[5] either by the nation of Israel or by the king, even though the creation theology of these ancient Hebrews is not in doubt? This question is especially pressing when we contrast this paucity of reference to God as Father in the Hebrew Scriptures with the prevalence of such usage of Father language in the surrounding ANE cultures beginning at least as early as the second millennium B.C.[6] For example, the king of the Hittites prays to Telephinus and says of him "Of every land you are Father (and) Mother" (in J. B. Pritchard, ed., *Ancient Near Eastern Texts* [ANET] 397). In a song to Marduk, Anu is proclaimed as "the great Father of the gods" (ANET 390). The moon god Sin is also addressed as "Father Nanna, lord Anshar, hero of the gods . . . Father and begetter of

---

4. Brueggemann, *Theology of the Old Testament*, p. 247.

5. A lack generally recognized. See Meye Thompson, *The Promise of the Father*, p. 39: "The relative infrequency of the term father for God does contrast sharply with the regular use of the term in the New Testament. But the scarcity of the term as over against the New Testament does not signal radical discontinuity with the presentation of God in the Old Testament."

6. See the discussion by T. Jacobsen, *The Treasures of Darkness: A History of Mesopotamian Religion* (New Haven: Yale University Press, 1976), pp. 225-26: "The truly new, the fundamentally new achievement of the second millennium was its genius in lighting upon a new metaphor truly suggestive of essential elements in the human response to the numinous experience. This parent metaphor, which saw the Numinous as a father or a mother significantly enhanced and deepened the sense of facinosum that was present already in the worship of the fertility gods. . . . It enhanced and deepened it by recognizing and expressing a personal relationship to the divine, a sense of attraction being reciprocal. Man who under the ruler metaphor was subject and slave, gained sonship."

the gods" (ANET 385-86). In Egypt Amun Re is also called the Father of the gods (ANET 365). This contrast has suggested to W. A. Van Gemeren that "Israel was surrounded by nations who held to a mythological understanding of a relationship between the worlds of the gods and men. In this context the writers of the OT cautiously referred to Yahweh as 'Father'; Yahweh is not El the father of 'the gods'. He is not Baal, the god of fertility. Yahweh is the Creator of everything and is sovereign (Lord, King, Ruler) over the nations."[7] This explanation is likely partially correct, but then why would the early Christians not have avoided such language as well, since they were all initially Jews, and since this Father language was still being applied in their day to numerous gods who begat other gods, not to mention to the emperor himself as divine? Perhaps one could hypothesize that since Christianity was a missionary religion, it actually looked for points of contact in its God language with that of the larger culture, whereas Hebrew God talk was primarily concerned with stressing what distinguished Yahweh from other deities. Nevertheless, the usage of surrounding cultures cannot entirely explain the absence of Father language in the OT.

It is the view of C. Seitz that one needs to take into account the perspectival difference in the use of the term "Father" in the OT and NT. In the older testament things are seen from the Father's point of view, whereas the Father is largely viewed from the Son's point of view in the NT. In other words, the "change . . . has less to do with matter of culture *or even something more personal or psychological,* and more to do with the appearance of the man Jesus and a change in perspective: from the Son to YHWH, who is referred to from that filial point of standing as 'Heavenly Father.'"[8] This is essentially the correct answer. It is Jesus himself who places the emphasis on God as Father, and this explains why the usage in the NT is so much more prevalent than in the OT.

Another answer sometimes offered up is that the Israelites did not have an intimate relationship with God in the same sort of familiar or

7. W. A. Van Gemeren, "Abba in the Old Testament," *Journal of the Evangelical Theological Society* 31 (1988): 385-98, here p. 392.

8. C. Seitz, *Word without End* (Grand Rapids: Eerdmans, 1998), p. 258.

familial terms as early Christians did. God was seen as the Holy One, truly transcendent, and therefore to some degree rather unapproachable. There is probably a measure of truth to this explanation since there is a strong emphasis in the OT on the holiness of God, but do we really want to say that the surrounding ANE cultures who regularly addressed some god as father envisioned their relationship with their deities as more intimate than that shared between Yahweh and the Israelites? Probably not.

Another possible answer would be that the sort of ethical monotheism we find in the OT cannot be simply compared with divine-human relationships in a polytheistic setting. In the latter case one could have some deities with which one was rather close in relationship, and others would be envisioned as more remote and transcendent. Ethical monotheism places a premium on an exclusive relationship between God and God's people, such that if the people are not faithful they have betrayed a covenant and indeed have invalidated the possibility of an intimate relationship by their immoral behavior (see, e.g., Jer. 3:19 above). There is then a possibility of moral distancing from the one and only God, a horrific prospect.

It will serve us well at this juncture to look again at the crucial story in Exodus of divine self-revelation. To anticipate our conclusions and give a synopsis of where this discussion is going, we will say that this Exodus story *does* suggest an intimate relationship between God and Moses in which the divine name is revealed, but the larger context also suggests that this was exceptional. Such a relationship was uncommon between God and individual Hebrews, or even the Israelites as a group. In part this was because of the lack of fidelity of many Israelites to the covenant. The OT texts previously cited suggest that God wished to have an intimate relationship with his people, but the language comes up usually in the very contexts that suggest the rebellion against or straying of God's people from that relationship.

Thus, the answer as to why God is not called Father more in the OT may also in part lie in the fact that God's people had not reached the stage in their relationship with God that Moses himself did, and therefore God did not yet fully reveal the divine character to Israel in those terms. Yahweh was prepared to relate to Israel in this way, but they were not prepared to respond in such terms. In fact, we notice in the later prophetic evidence that Father language is used to chastise Israel from moving away from the possibility of such an intimate relationship. Yet still only in this later prophetic literature is God really begun to be revealed as Father, and this progression continues on into the intertestamental literature, as we shall see. It is as if God increasingly attempts to reveal the divine nature in intimate terms, not just to individuals but to the chosen people as a whole, but the response in prayer and praise using the Father language is generally lacking. Let us consider the Exodus text first.

The material in Exodus 3 has been a storm center of controversy in OT scholarship on various counts. Are we dealing with a "call narrative"? Are we dealing with a vision? How is the divine name to be interpreted? These are just some of the questions the text raises. In the first place it seems that in the burning bush story we are dealing with a call narrative of the same ilk we find in Judges 3 or Jeremiah 1. Basically this sort of narrative involves a conversation between Yahweh or one of his messengers and a particular individual. In fact, Ex. 3:1–4:17 could be said to be a greatly expanded form of this sort of narrative. N. Habel outlines this call narrative as follows: (1) the divine confrontation — vv. 1-4a; (2) the introductory word — vv. 4b-9; (3) the commission — v. 10; (4) the objections — v. 11; (5) the reassurance — v. 12a; (6) the sign — v. 12b.[9] To this, however, we must add that vv. 13ff. continue the litany of objections of various sorts until finally God gets angry (4:14) and settles the matter once and for all. Notice how reluctant Moses actually is. He tries to excuse himself by saying he is unequipped, unknowledgeable, unable to cope with rejection, and inexperienced; and it becomes increasingly clear as the narrative goes on that he is simply unwilling to do as asked. Here is not what one would call an eager volunteer in the service of Yahweh.

The setting of the story finds Moses out in the Sinai peninsula tending sheep; he appears to be looking for better pasture when he comes

---

9. N. Habel, "The Form and Significance of the Call Narratives," *Zeitschrift für die alttestamentliche Wissenschaft* (1965): 297-323.

to Mt. Horeb which seems to be just another name for Mt. Sinai, and is already here called the mountain of God. This perhaps looks forward to later events to take place here. It is doubtless no accident that the very mountain where God will reveal his will and presence to his people later is where he reveals his will and presence to Moses now. Moses is simply minding his father-in-law's business, not seeking any close encounters with the deity. Verse 2 tells us that the *malak Yahweh* appears to Moses. Various commentators through the ages have suggested that this being is in fact just God manifesting the divine presence (cf., e.g., Gen. 18:1; 19:1). In other words, it is not merely God's messenger but God in person who speaks to Moses. Thus we are perhaps dealing with a theophany rather than just an angelophany here.

Notice that this text does not say that the *malak Yahweh* appeared in any sort of form here, but in a flame of fire in a bush. Fire is also a symbol of God's presence when God descends on Sinai before the people and Moses in Ex. 19:18. The peculiarity of seeing a bush burn without being consumed intrigues Moses and so he draws closer. God's presence as a flame would seem to imply God's holiness, purifying force, and perhaps his miraculous power (cf. v. 5). Any being who can set a bush on fire without destroying it is a unique being. This event does not seem to be a supernatural vision (contrast Ezek. 1), but rather a miraculous occurrence happening outside of Moses' psyche.[10]

God calls Moses by name twice, indicating a certain urgency; Moses responds immediately, "Here I am." Throughout this passage while Moses complains about his inability as a public speaker he shows himself more than capable of carrying on a dialogue with God at length. Ex. 3:5 should be translated "stop coming near (as you are doing)." God does not want Moses to experience premature ministerial burnout! Actually the point is that Moses is not yet ready to come into God's presence. He must first be prepared and know with Whom he is dealing. This he finds out in v. 6. The place is called holy ground because God is there, not because it is inherently sacred or hallowed ground.

10. For a useful caution against overpsychologizing this story see B. Childs, *Exodus* (Philadelphia: Westminster, 1974), pp. 72-73.

This is in fact the first occurrence of the word "holy" in the Bible, and it is linked with God's presence. But God not only is holy, God requires holiness of his people. The taking off of sandals may be because they were dirty, or we may be dealing with an ANE practice of taking off various articles of clothing in a god's presence. Sumerian priests, for example, performed their tasks naked, while Israelite priests wore only a modicum of clothing (Ex. 20:26).

Ex. 3:6 refers either to the "God of your father" or the "God of your fathers." In either case the point is that Moses will not be called upon to reveal to the Israelites some new God that Amram worshiped. Rather he is to speak to them in the name of the God of their own patriarchs, at which time God will reveal the divine being more fully and by a personal name (Yahweh). When Moses suddenly realizes he is in God's presence he hides his face, for he is afraid of looking directly upon God (cf. 1 Kings 19:13; Is. 6:2 on this gesture as a sign of recognition and reverence).

The next major segment of the story is found in 3:7-12. Beginning with v. 7 God explains that he has not ignored the cries of his people. Rather, God has both heard them and come down to do something about their suffering. God cares so much that he has come from heaven to intervene on their behalf. The story makes quite clear that it is God, not Moses, who is the prime rescuer of his own people — "I have come down to rescue them . . . and bring them up out of the land." Not only so, but he plans on the positive side to provide a homeland for them, a land currently inhabited by various peoples and groups. Furthermore, it's not just any land but a good and broad land "oozing with milk and honey." The image here is of a rich pastureland that produces cows or goats or sheep with bulging udders and milk leaking from their teats. Honey is a reference to the product of bees, which in turn implies a land of flowers and trees with pollen and nectar. We are not talking about subsistence farming in the desert.

Up until v. 10 Moses may have been thinking he was dreaming, but if so this verse brings him back down to earth — "I am sending you to Pharaoh . . . to bring my people out." Moses' initial response is understandable — he is overwhelmed. It is too great a task for one who is now a simple shepherd and in any case he is unworthy of such a job. "Who am I that I should go to Pharaoh?" Moses is probably not making excuses yet. He simply sees himself as inadequate to the task. But it is not the adequacy of Moses or his worthiness that is at issue. Since God who is fully adequate and worthy will be with him, Moses' own shortcomings will not prevent God from using him. God gives a twofold answer: (1) "I will be with you," perhaps a play on the name Yahweh as it is explained in vv. 14-15; (2) there is the offering of a sign.

Signs are a common feature of OT stories and there are several sorts of sign narratives: (1) a narrative where a sign, whether a miracle or a wonder or special event, confirms the truthfulness of God's word; and (2) narratives where the sign continues what will yet happen in the future but has been spoken about in the present.[11] The problem with Ex. 3:12 is that it doesn't quite fit either of these paradigms. The confirmation comes after the prophesied and commissioned events have already happened, not merely after they have been foretold. Thus Ex. 3:12 is anomalous. There seems to be a reason for this — God is expecting Moses to have faith in his word, that it will come true. The proof that it is God who has sent Moses is that one day he will be back at Mt. Horeb worshiping. The realization of that event will show that God was with Moses all along. Moses has seen God's power in the bush, so the additional sign at this point in time should not have been necessary. The occurrence of that event confirms the identity and reality of the Lord who speaks to Moses.

Ex. 3:13-15 brings us to the passage that is of greatest concern for this study. What is God's name? What does the name mean or signify? What sort of question is Moses asking? Bearing in mind that v. 12 says "I will be with you," in v. 14 we have the same form of the verb *hayah*. Notice that we do not have in v. 14 *ani asher ani* but a paranomastic use of the verb *hayah*. This suggests on the one hand that we ought not to translate the phrase "I am that I am" as if it were an ontological statement, a statement about God's being, but rather we seem to be being told something about God's activity or self-revelation in his

---

11. Childs, *Exodus*, pp. 56-58.

activity. The focus then is not on God's being a self-contained, self-existent being.

Normally when God was going to act or had just revealed himself, he was given a new title or name (cf. Gen. 16:13). Notice that Moses does not say "Who are you, or who shall I say that you are?" Rather, he asks what he should say when it is inquired: "What *(mah)* is his name?" which seems to mean "What new revelation have you received from God?" "Under what new title has God appeared to you?"[12]

Moses' question is posed not merely as a hypothetical one, but as the natural and expected reaction of the oppressed Israelites. Authenticity of Moses' mission is linked to a revelation of the divine name confirming that God is going to do something. Notice that vv. 14b-15 do not suggest that *eyeh asher eyeh* is taken as a *refusal* by God to respond or to reveal himself. It cannot be a totally enigmatic response. Furthermore, vv. 14b-15 should be seen as parallel explanations or responses and v. 15 is clear enough. It is the God of their fathers who is speaking to them and promising this, and *that* God is already in part known to them.

The verbal form *eyeh* is an imperfect that indicates a kind of action, not primarily a time of action — in this case an action yet to be completed. Thus it is an action that could have begun in the past, or begins in the present or will begin in the future, but will take some time to be completed. In the case of v. 12 we know that the sense must be futuritive. This suggests we should see it the same way here.

It seems probable that the Tetragrammaton YHWH is a shortening of the whole phrase *eyeh asher eyeh* into a personal name. The clause contains the necessary vowels, and the consonants are quite close. Clearly *eyeh* is given as a form of God's name in v. 14b. To be sure, this is a punning on the name, a play on words, but it does reveal something about the name. God then is not speaking about what God is in the divine essence, but rather what Yahweh is or will be in relationship to his people — in his self-revelation. This comports nicely with the fact that the Israelites' reason for asking about the name has to do with a great

12. See R. A. Cole, *Exodus* (London: Tyndale Press, 1973), pp. 69-70.

need. They need to know not merely that God exists, but that God does and will soon act on their behalf. S. Driver notes:

> The expression *I will be* is a historical formula; it refers, not to what God will be in Himself; it is no predication regarding his essential nature, but one regarding what He will approve Himself to others, regarding what he will show Himself to be to those in covenant with Him, as by His providential guidance of His people, and the teaching of His prophets, His character and attributes were more and more fully unfolded to them.[13]

The formula thus means: I will be understood by my future acts and revelation. This makes very good sense indeed, for in all the subsequent accounts of Israelite history God is to be known as the one who brought Israel out of Egypt (Ex. 20:2). "The revelation of the name therefore is not merely a deep theological truth; it is a call to a response of faith by Moses and by Israel."[14]

This means that Israel's God is a God of history, not a God who created and wound up the universe like a clock and then left it to wind down on its own. Yahweh is the one who keeps intervening in human history. Thus this naming is in fact a call for Moses to have faith. As in v. 12 so in v. 14 God is saying to Moses and so to Israel, "I will reveal myself through these future acts of redemption and you will know me by them, as the God who delivers you out of Egypt." In short, it is true even of God that you shall know the tree by the fruit it bears.

Finally, it should be noted that we may see in vv. 14-15 an interplay between the God who will be and the God who has been for the patriarchs. It is this same God who will rescue the people of God. To remind Israel that Yahweh is the God of the patriarchs is to remind them of what he did for Abraham, Isaac, Jacob, and Joseph. They are called then not to a blind faith in a God who someday may act and so reveal the di-

13. S. Driver, *The Book of Exodus* (Cambridge: Cambridge University Press, 1953), pp. 40-41.

14. Cole, *Exodus,* p. 70.

vine nature or character. Rather they are called to renew their faith in one who has always acted for the people of God. Thus Yahweh is indeed a very personal name for the God of the patriarchs. He is the God who leads them into their future, going before them with pillars of smoke and fire.[15]

Thus this passage suggests that God will be known in what God will yet do — the divine nature being made plain by divine actions. It is not merely that the name Yahweh suggests that God is the Living One, though that is true, but that God is a God of revelation, and that therefore the future revelations and actions will further disclose the name and nature of God. Patience and faith are required on the part of Moses before he can know God truly and intimately. God not only has a plan for his people, God has a story; and part of the story is this: God will choose when and where the divine name will be revealed through actions and speech. This narrative then suggests not only intimacy between God and his people, but also an ongoing story with more yet to be revealed. It suggests a set of circumstances in which God's people would look forward to and expect God to continue to progressively reveal the divine character and plan and purposes. One of the ways that was to happen was by the drawing of analogies between God's activities and that of a human father, and even the naming of God as Father, the creator and sustainer of a people who relates to those people in an intimate, even if sometimes intimidatingly open and frank fashion.[16]

The further development of the Jewish use of Father language for God brings us to texts especially in the intertestamental Wisdom literature, for example, Wis. 14:3; Sir. 23:1, 4; 51:10, but also 3 Macc. 6:3, 8. Since it appears that both 3 Maccabees and Wisdom were originally composed in Greek, we are not talking here about evidence for the use of *abba* for God before the time of Jesus, but more broadly we have evidence for

---

15. Childs, *Exodus*, pp. 60ff.

16. It is of course true, and important, that the Father language sometimes shows up in texts where the actual subject is not physical creation but rather the re-creation or redemption of Israel as a people. In such texts it of course does not refer to actual begetting but rather to a process of rescuing and forming a people. On this see Meye Thompson, *The Promise of the Father*, pp. 41-43.

some sort of Father language used of God. Especially striking among these texts is Wis. 14:3, where God is actually addressed as Father. This may suggest a growing tendency, first noted in the later prophetic corpus, toward using such language of God, even in prayer. As for the evidence from Sirach, in Sir. 51:10 God is called *abi* not *abba* in the Hebrew text, and in the Greek version of Sir. 23:4 we have *kurie pater*. But it is important that the evidence in Sirach bears witness to a preponderance of examples where God is said to be the Father of individuals (cf. 10:12; 32:13; 33:13; 47:8).[17] This trend will continue in the NT literature.

When we discover in some of the Qumran fragments (4Q 371 and 372) evidence for the addressing of God as *abi* (not *abba*) we may begin to think of a growing trend in Jewish culture in the direction of addressing God as Father. Yet it must be remembered that *abi* is in fact a rather formal way of addressing God. It means "my father," unlike *abba* which appears to be a more intimate and informal form of address.[18] The Aramaic usage of Jesus remains without parallel.[19]

There is also material to be found in the later Targums and in the Talmud that points to a growing use of Father language for God in early Judaism. The texts in question are B. T. Taan. 23b; Targ. Ps. 89:27; and Targ. Mal. 2:10, with the first of these being the most important of the lot. Honi ha Nehba was a Jewish sage who lived near the end of the first century B.C. B. T. Taan. 23b tells the tale of how during a drought some school children came to Honi crying out *"abba, abba, habh lan mitra"* which means "father, father, give us rain." After this plea Honi interceded with the Almighty, praying "Master of the world, grant it for the sake of these who are not yet able to distinguish between an *abba* who has power to give rain and an *abba* who has not." In fact, God is not addressed here as *abba;* rather we are dealing with a play on words, so characteristic of Jewish wisdom literature. God is addressed here as Master of the world. Nonetheless, this text is important because it shows us that small children could address a teacher as *abba*, though it

---

17. See Meye Thompson, *The Promise of the Father*, p. 51.

18. On this matter and on Jesus' use of *abba* see the next chapter.

19. Meye Thompson, *The Promise of the Father*, p. 50.

was surely more common to use it of a parent. With this text, as with the next two as well, we must be cautious since there is the possible problem of anachronism — a latter way of speaking being predicated of an early period.

Targ. Mal. 2:10 does not invoke God as *abba* or father, but Targ. Ps. 89:27 is more intriguing. Here God promises the future anointed Davidic king that he will call on God saying "You are *abba* to me, my God." It is difficult to know if this tradition actually goes back to the time of Jesus or is from a later period. The latter seems more likely. Nevertheless, what we learn from this text is that a unique person, the Davidic messiah, will be allowed one day to address God as *abba*. This is apparently because the Davidic king, as we have already seen in this discussion, was thought of as God's son in some special sense (cf. Ps. 89:19-37; Ps. 2:7-9).

Conclusions

What may we conclude from this cursory exploration of God-as-Father language in Jewish literature? First, it seems quite apparent that one can *not* maintain that there is no evidence of intimacy between God and the chosen people in this literature. From God's side of the equation, there are repeated attempts to treat the chosen people as a good father would his children. The Father language seems to come up especially when the issue is the creating of the chosen people.

This brings up an important point. Meye Thompson claims that the characterizing of God as Father is not derived from attributes that are inherent or specific to the male gender "but rather from the specific set of functions which were appropriate to fathers in that Israelite culture."[20] But this is not totally correct. To the extent the term is used to describe God as a begetter rather than a conceiver of creation or creatures there is a gender-specific component to the term. Only males beget, only females conceive. This is not to say YHWH is said to be a male

---

20. Meye Thompson, *The Promise of the Father*, p. 54.

when he is called Father, but it is to say that the terminology "Father" does sometimes refer to some gender-specific activities. In other words, in such cases other terminology such as "Mother" would not be equally suitable. We will see that this is also true in the NT where God is described as the Father of the Son, including in terms that make clear that Jesus did not have a human father who begat him (see Mt. 1 and Lk. 2).

Second, we must also continue to stress that the addressing of God in intimate terms using Father language is exceedingly rare in the OT, and overall one gets the impression that there were mainly special individuals who had what one would call a personal relationship with God, if such a relationship entails addressing God as Father or in equivalent terms. Yet we must also note that there seems to have been an increasing degree of comfort with the use of Father language for God as we get to the late prophetic and then the intertestamental period. We must further stress that there is no clear evidence in the early Jewish literature for praying to God as *abba* prior to the time of Jesus. Addressing God as "my Father" is a more formal sort of address than *abba*. God as creator of a people and as parental guardian and guide of them are the images that come to light from the use of Father language in these texts. As we turn to the NT data we will discover a remarkable proliferation of the use of Father language, and many new aspects to the profile of God suggested by the use of this language. God's story takes a dramatic new turn when Jesus the Son appears on the scene.

QUESTIONS

1. As Hebrews 1:1ff. states, the revelation of God was partial until Jesus came. For this reason we should not expect a full discussion of the Trinity in the Old Testament. Considering the texts discussed so far and the image of God put forth in the OT, answer the following questions.

   A. Why is it important to read the preliminary material of the OT in the light of its sequel, the NT?

B. How does the partial understanding of God in the OT influence one's understanding of the NT?

C. How can statements about God be held as true if only part of the picture is given?

D. Why would God choose to provide a partial and gradual revelation until Jesus?

2. The discussion of chapter one focuses on the OT relationship between God and his people. From Jer. 3:19 one gains a clear understanding that God had hoped for a father/child relationship with Israel — a relationship that was not fulfilled.

A. Compare and contrast characteristics that are noted in chapter one with those commonly associated with human fathers.

B. How does our relationship to God compare to a father/child relationship?

C. How does one's own relationship with one's biological father influence one's understanding and reception of God?

3. In Exodus 3, the name of God is given to Moses as "I am that I am." This seems to be more of a statement about God's activity or self-revelation than a statement about his being. If you are able, use your knowledge of Hebrew to create a short translation and exegesis of the passage, then use it to answer the following questions.

A. What is the significance of receiving God's name?

B. How does this statement of self-revelation relate to Jesus' "I am" statements in John? See: John 6:35; 8:12; 10:7, 9, 11; 11:25; 14:6; 15:15; etc.

C. How do these passages shed light upon the understanding of the Trinitarian relationship?

4. As a sovereign God, God could have chosen to predestine our lives but instead gave people freedom of choice. As a result God's inter-

vention in history seems limited. However, he chose to intervene through Moses as well as other prophets and situations in the OT.

A. Why does God choose to use human beings or messengers rather than his own power?

B. Was Jesus different? If so, how? If not, how?

C. Does God still use human beings/messengers/prophets today? If so, how are these different than those used in the OT?

CHAPTER TWO

The Promising Father

—◁◁◊▷▷—

Thus far we have seen that there was some precedent for the use of father language of God in early Judaism. But what we did not find in this literature are any of the following things: (1) the use of *abba* as an address for God in prayer; (2) the regular use of "Father" or *abba* by a particular historical individual to indicate his personal relationship to God; (3) any adequate historical explanation (based in pre-Christian usage of Father language) for the astonishing proliferation of Father language for God in the NT documents, which were all, or almost all, written by first-century Jewish Christians; (4) any adequate explanation for why the use of Father language in early Christianity seems to have increased from the time of the writing of the earliest Gospel (Mark — which has only four references to God as Father) to the time of the writing of the later Gospels (particularly Matthew, which has more than 30 references to God as Father, and John, which has some 120 references). All of these factors point to a conclusion that the early Jewish context by itself cannot explain the phenomena we find in the NT when it comes to the use of the term "Father" or *abba* for God.[1] The issue of discontinuity

1. We would like to express appreciation for the foundational and helpful work done by M. Meye Thompson on Father language for God in the NT in her recent study *The Promise of the Father* (Louisville: Westminster/John Knox, 2000). This chapter is indebted to her work in that study at various points, even when, in some cases, we have certainly differed with her judgments.

with earlier Jewish practice must be balanced against the evidence for continuity, and, to anticipate our conclusions, the emphasis so far as the NT presents the matter should lie on discontinuity with previous Jewish practice. Something new transpired when Jesus came on the scene so far as the use of Father language by early Jews is concerned.

I. Jesus, *Abba,* and the Impact of the Son's Relationship to the Father

We hinted in the last chapter at a probable explanation for the difference in usage of Father language in early Judaism and early Christianity (both in frequency and to some degree in character), and it has to do with Jesus. As Seitz has argued, in the older testament things are seen from the Father's point of view, whereas the Father is largely viewed from the Son's point of view in the NT. In other words, the "change . . . has less to do with matter of culture *or even something more personal or psychological,* and more to do with the appearance of the man Jesus and a change in perspective: from The Son to YHWH, who is referred to from that filial point of standing as 'Heavenly Father.'"[2]

This is essentially the correct answer. It is Jesus himself that places the emphasis on God as Father, and this explains why the usage in the NT is so much more prevalent than in the OT. More importantly, it is the new perspective of seeing the Father through the eyes of the Son and on the basis of the Son's relationship to the Father that explains what we find in the NT. Such a relationship is in a limited way presaged by the language used of the king to describe his relationship with God, for example in Ps. 2. In other words, it is the special relationship Israel's Messiah, or Anointed One, was to have with God that provides some precedent for Jesus' and early Christianity's usage, not the occasional and more general usage of Father imagery to describe the relationship of God to Israel writ large.[3] Christians came to believe that one comes

---

2. C. Seitz, *Word without End* (Grand Rapids: Eerdmans, 1998), p. 258.

3. Contra Meye Thompson, *The Promise of the Father,* p. 79, who argues that "Jesus

to the Father through Jesus the Son in part because Jesus believed he had a special sonship relationship with God the Father. Jesus acted out the drama of being God's anointed one and mediated this new relationship with the Father. Jesus did not see himself as Israel, but rather as Israel's redeemer, and indeed as the agent and emissary of the Father in this regard.

We must begin then with the story of the Son's relationship to the Father as lived out by the historical Jesus himself, before we consider the various canonical perspectives on this matter. This means we must go back and consider the older arguments of J. Jeremias about Jesus' use of *abba* as well as some of the critique of those arguments.

It was the argument of Jeremias that "the complete novelty and uniqueness of *Abba* as an address to God in the prayers of Jesus shows that it expresses the heart of Jesus' relationship to God."[4] Jeremias basically maintained not that Jesus' view of God was entirely novel, but that his mode of address to God was novel because his relationship with God was distinctive. In other words, some texts that manifested a corporate relationship to God (e.g., later rabbinic prayers addressing God as "our Father") were not true parallels to Jesus' usage, nor was the general use of Father imagery to describe some activity of God, rather than the personal addressing of God as Father. For example, about a text such as B. T. Taan. 23b where Honi draws an analogy between a

---

understood God first as father of the people of Israel, and his own relationship to God in and from that framework. . . ." Meye Thompson fails to grasp the radicality of Jesus' own ministry and mission. She argues (p. 84) that "to trust God as Father is thus not to come to a new intimacy with God but, rather, to renew one's trust in the God of Israel." This is simply incorrect. Jesus believed Israel was basically lost and needed to be redeemed. He, like the Baptist, called for radical repentance and warned of judgment, which one's ethnic heritage would not protect one from if one did not repent. The new eschatological covenant was not seen as a mere renewing of the old one. Repentance, discipleship, taking on the yoke of the new covenant indeed meant coming to a new intimacy with God that allowed one to address God as *abba*, once one is enabled and prompted to do so by the eschatological Spirit which Jesus promised.

4. J. Jeremias, *New Testament Theology: The Proclamation of Jesus* (New York: Scribner's, 1971), p. 67. See also especially his *The Prayers of Jesus* (Philadelphia: Fortress Press, 1967).

human father and God using the term *abba*, Jeremias stresses that God is addressed by Honi not as *abba*, but as Master of the universe.

In the early form of Jeremias's argument about Jesus' use of *abba* he postulated that Jesus adopted the language of a tiny child addressing his Father (e.g., as if *abba* meant something like "Daddy"). To his credit Jeremias later changed his mind about this, because he saw that it was a form of address used even by an adult son of his father.[5] Thus while J. Barr was quite right to stress that *abba* doesn't mean Daddy, this shouldn't be taken as an adequate criticism of the mature form of Jeremias's argument.[6] The term *abba* is clearly enough an intimate way of addressing God using family language, whether by a child or an adult, and as such is less formal than addressing God simply as God or Lord. Jeremias's main point is that Jesus' choice of this term reveals Jesus' awareness of his special relationship with God, and it is fair to say that this point withstands the recent critiques of his argument.

At this juncture several facts need to be highlighted. First, whenever Jesus directly addresses God in the Gospels he always speaks to God as Father with one telling exception — when he quotes Ps. 22 ("My God, my God, why have you forsaken me?") from the cross (see Mk. 15:34). To put matters the other way around, Jesus never addresses God as King or Master or by other terms familiar to early Jews. This phenomenon requires explanation. Second, at perhaps the paramount crisis moment in Jesus' ministry, when he was in the garden of Gethsemane praying for guidance, according to our earliest Gospel Jesus addressed God as *abba* (Mk. 14:36). The setting suggests an earnest pleading with God in the most intimate of terms.[7]

In her recent study of Father language in the NT Meye Thompson argues "even if Jesus' use of the vernacular in prayer were the decisive

5. See Jeremias's self correction on this in his *NT Theology*, p. 67.

6. See J. Barr, "Abba Isn't Daddy," *Journal of Theological Studies* 39 (1988): 28-47. Barr recognizes that Jeremias did not maintain that Jesus called God "Daddy."

7. The fact that Luke and Matthew in the parallels to this text omit the term *abba* while retaining its translation as "Father" probably tells us more about their audience's (or their own?) lack of knowledge of Aramaic, than of the authors' reluctance to characterize Jesus' prayer language in these terms.

issue, it is still curious that no one is ever shown as objecting to Jesus' use of abba because of its startling connotations."[8] The problem with this argument, besides the fact that it is an argument from silence, is that when we are dealing with *abba* as an address to God we are talking about Jesus' prayer language (and indeed in Gethsemane his private and personal prayer language) not his form of public discourse with anyone other than his disciples.

Third, Jesus alone is depicted in the Gospels as speaking of God as "my Father," and outside the Gospels the phrase "my Father" appears only on Jesus' lips (Rev. 2:27; 3:5; 3:21). Jesus does not pray *with* his disciples "our Father"; rather he teaches his disciples to do so as part of *their* corporate prayer life. Furthermore, what evidence we have suggests that early Christians only began to pray to God as *abba* as a result of having received the Holy Spirit who prompts such prayer (cf. Rom. 8:15-16; Gal. 4:6).[9] In other words, there is a distinction made between the prayer life of Jesus and that of the disciples during the ministry. Only Jesus is actually shown as addressing God as *abba* during his ministry. But when the disciples received the eschatological Spirit they too were enabled and prompted to do so.[10] Fourth, "Father" is used for God in multiple sources in the Gospels (Mark, Q, M, and L). In some of this material, particularly the Q saying in Mt. 11:25-27/Lk. 10:21-22, the intimacy of the Father-Son relationship is stressed. They share knowledge that others do not have unless the Son dispenses it. In Mk. 8:38 the Son of Man

8. Meye Thompson, *The Promise of the Father*, p. 30.

9. These are the earliest references in the NT to praying to God as *abba,* and both clearly link such prayer to the Spirit and to having some kind of special status as a result of the work of Christ and one's relationship of faith to him. We will say a good deal more about these texts shortly. See pp. 29-35 below.

10. Here Meye Thompson, *The Promise of the Father*, p. 65, is surely right: ". . . a more plausible hypothesis, in light of the restricted use of Father in Paul and its virtual disappearance in Acts [only in Acts 1:5, 8 and 2:33] and other New Testament books, is that the usage was deemed characteristic of Jesus and thus was taken over in continuity with Jesus' own usage. Hence the persistent use of 'our Father' and the absence of 'my Father' from the rest of the New Testament may suggest that both could be traced back to Jesus, with 'our Father' as a form of address commended to his followers and 'my Father' limited to Jesus himself."

comes in the glory of his Father. What these facts highlight is that there is strong reason both to believe that Jesus addressed God as Father and that he taught his followers to do so, but at the same time he distinguished his own relationship to the Father from that of his followers.

Another helpful aspect of Jeremias's treatment of Jesus' use of *abba* is that he stresses that one needs to read Jesus' God language in the eschatological context of Jesus' general theological discourse. In other words, Jesus believed that God was acting as Father and redeemer of his children in a final and definitive way through Jesus' own ministry. Jeremias puts it this way: "In Jesus' eyes, being a child of God is not a gift of creation, but an eschatological gift of salvation."[11] In other words, Jesus is not simply perpetuating the earlier Jewish usage of Father language for God. Jesus believes that such a relationship with God comes through a positive response to Jesus' ministry in the form of discipleship to Jesus. Meye Thompson concludes from this that Jeremias is urging "It was not a new conception of God that prompted Jesus' use of Father. Instead Jesus' conviction that God's eschatological salvation was now proffered through his own person and work led him, conscious of this distinctive role and of his unique relationship to God, to address God, personally and directly, as abba."[12] Here it is apposite to remember Jer. 31:9 where God laments the broken relationship between Israel and God, a relationship which, if healthy, should have led them to call God Father. Jeremias then grounded the *abba* language in Jesus' unique filial consciousness, and the passing on of that language to his followers was grounded in the eschatological situation that Jesus believed he was inaugurating.[13]

---

11. Jeremias, *NT Theology*, p. 181.

12. Meye Thompson, *The Promise of the Father*, p. 32.

13. This is an important distinction that Meye Thompson does not seem to fully recognize. Jesus did not see himself as one of those God was now redeeming, thus warranting his own use of *abba* language. Rather, he saw himself as the one who stood on God's side doing the redeeming. Thus *abba* for him reflects an intimate relationship intact throughout the ministry, at least until the cross, while *abba* for his followers indicates they have been redeemed through the eschatological ministry of Jesus and were now able to appropriately address God as *abba,* as Jesus always could.

God is addressed in intimate terms by the disciples after Easter because God has drawn near through Jesus in a definitive way, creating a familial relationship with them that did not fully exist before Jesus came on the scene. In other words, while there is OT discussion about God's longing to have such a familial relationship with his people and about his intent to redeem his people in a full and final way, it is apparently Jesus and his disciples' view that this did not transpire prior to the ministry of Jesus. It is primarily the discontinuity with the past situation of the relationship between God and human beings, rather than the continuity, that Jesus and this language are emphasizing. Paul's placing of the discussion of *abba* in the context of a discussion of the final salvific work of Christ and the Spirit reflects the impact of Jesus' usage of *abba*.[14]

We may conclude then that there is more than sufficient evidence that Jesus himself prayed to God and addressed God as *abba* or Father. This seems to have reflected the intimacy of his relationship with God. Thus, while we may not be able to talk about Jesus' subjective *experience* of God,[15] it is clear from the Gethsemane narrative that Jesus had an intimate *relationship* with God, so intimate that he could ask God to let him bypass the cross! He could plead with him as a Son to a Father, addressing him as dearest Father (= *abba*).[16] We may also conclude that

14. If we may use an analogy, it is rather like looking at the enormous meteor crater in Arizona, in which there are only small traces of the meteor itself. The size of the crater, however, clearly bears witness to the original size of the meteor. Though the evidence for Jesus' use of *abba* in particular in the Gospels is not plentiful, nevertheless its importance can be judged by its impact on his earliest followers. Paul was certainly one of those earliest followers, converted within a few years of Jesus' death.

15. For example, we could not say in Schleiermacherian terms that he had a "feeling of absolute dependency on God," since Jesus does not usually discourse on his feelings or his subjective religious experiences. Yet a case could be made that the temptation narrative in Q and the baptismal narrative in Mark reflect Jesus' relating of visionary experiences to his disciples, as might the saying "I saw Satan fall like lightning from the sky."

16. Meye Thompson, *The Promise of the Father*, pp. 56ff., seems sometimes not to be able to distinguish what can be said about a relationship Jesus had with God, which has some public dimensions, and what can be said about his subjective experiences. One's relationship with God is a larger reality than one's subjective impressions or experiences garnered while in that relationship.

the best explanation for the nature and frequency of Father language in the NT is that this phenomenon reflects the impact of Jesus' God language, Jesus' relationship with God, and the way Jesus instructed his disciples to speak about and relate to God. But can we say more? Let us consider a few examples from Mark and from Q that may reveal to us something of how the historical Jesus viewed the Father.

There are only four references to God as Father in our earliest Gospel, yet they are all revealing. We learn, for example, from Mk. 8:38 that Jesus believed that God was a glorious being, and that the Son of Man would one day come in that glory. From Mk. 11:25 we learn that God is a forgiving being and that we should emulate God's behavior. The implication of Mk. 13:32 is that God is an all-knowing being; he even knows the timing of the second coming. Lastly, from Mk. 14:36 we learn that God has a will and a plan for human beings, including for the life of Jesus. We also learn, interestingly enough, that Jesus' own will or desire could at times be at variance with that of the Father. The image of God we gain from these brief references is of a powerful, all-knowing God who is compassionate and working for the salvation of humankind.

The Q material that likely goes back to Jesus adds a bit more to this portrait of the Father. Mt. 11:25-27/Lk. 10:21-22 suggests that God shares with his Son certain intimate knowledge, and indeed this saying suggests that the way to know the Father is through receiving the revelation of who the Father is from the Son. Jesus is portrayed as the one who mediates the knowledge of God and the blessings of God. He himself is not the recipient of the OT promises of God, especially the promise that God can be known by his people, but rather the one who fulfills them or bestows them. Mt. 7:9-11/Lk. 11:11-13 suggests that God cares deeply for his children and provides for them.

To this we could add the portrait of the Father painted by Jesus in the parable of the vineyard in Mk. 12:1-12.[17] The Father is seen as the absentee owner of the vineyard (= Israel) who sends various emissaries (= prophets) to lay claim on the vineyard for the Father. The last of

---

17. On the authenticity of this parable see Ben Witherington III, *The Christology of Jesus* (Minneapolis: Fortress, 1990), pp. 213-14.

these emissaries is the Son. The issue of inheritance laws comes into play but should not be pushed too far, for technically the Son would only inherit the property after the Father died. The issue here then is the inappropriate response of the vineyard workers to Jesus, who by rights had a claim on the vineyard. Implied in the parable is the unique relationship Jesus had with the Father, seeing himself as God's only (begotten) Son and as God's last emissary to his people.

Most scholars also believe that the parable of the prodigal son found in Lk. 15:11-32 goes back to Jesus. This parable is not about Jesus, but rather about the forgiving Father. The Father is one prepared to receive the prodigal back if he repents, as is the case in this parable. The Father is not, however, portrayed here as the ultimately indulgent parent who forgives without repentance and who is incapable of tough love. The parable is after all about the return of the prodigal once he came to his senses, not about the seeking out of the lost (unlike the two earlier parables in Lk. 15).

If we put all these insights together, a compelling picture emerges of the Father whom Jesus knew intimately and spoke of. One of the major themes must be the intimate relationship depicted between the Father and Jesus. For Jesus he is *abba,* whose will and word is final. But this Father is no harsh unforgiving figure. To the contrary, the Father's active caring for and compassion on his people, even to the point of forgiving them their sins, is a repeated theme.[18] The Father is also one

---

18. Consider the noteworthy comments of feminist theologian Elizabeth A. Johnson, *Consider Jesus: Waves of Renewal in Christology* (New York: Crossroad, 1990), p. 57: "From the way Jesus talked about God and enacted the reign of God, it is obvious that he had a special and original experience of God as intimate, close, and tremendously compassionate over human suffering and sin. Out of that experience Jesus surfaced a name for God, namely *Abba.* . . . Jesus' own personal experience of God as close and compassionate led him to name God in his very intimate way, *Abba.* The name evokes the power of a very close relationship between Jesus and the One he names this way. Furthermore, Jesus teaches others to call God *Abba,* encouraging them to trust God the way little children trust a good parent to take care of them, be compassionate over their weakness, and stand guard against those who would harm them. Jesus' *Abba* experience is at the heart of the matter, the dynamism behind his preaching the reign of God and his typical way of acting. God *Abba* was the passion of his life."

who has chosen to relate to his people through his Son, who both reveals the Father to people and comes as an emissary to implement the Father's will in the vineyard, which is to say amongst God's people. One comes to, and comes to know, the Father and the Father's will through the Son, the final emissary to God's people. It is fully warranted to conclude that the prevalence of the use of Father language for God in the early church comes from Jesus' own use of such language, and more to the point, comes from Jesus' own intimate and special relationship with the Father, which set him apart from other and early Jews in important ways. The primary context out of which one ought to read Jesus' statements about the Father is not just the degree of intimacy with the Father that set him apart, but the unique relational role he played as the Father's only Son. As we shall now see, the impact on the early church of both the language and this relationship with the Father was enormous.

II. Paul on the Father of the Lord Jesus Christ

The earliest written documents in the NT are, according to the vast majority of scholars, Paul's letters. These letters then give us the earliest windows on the faith of the early Christians and particularly on their relationship with God. It is telling that in the NT as a whole, including the Pauline corpus, the term *theos,* God, with only a handful of exceptions always refers to the Father. In six or seven cases *theos* does refer to the Son (e.g., probably in Rom. 9:5), and in no cases does it refer to the Spirit or to the Trinity as a whole. This is not surprising since the earliest Christians were all Jewish monotheists, and probably all of the NT authors were as well, with the possible exception of Luke, who may have been a Gentile.[19] We must bear these facts in mind when we examine the Father language in Paul.

---

19. Even in his case, his extensive knowledge of the Greek OT, the Septuagint (LXX), suggests he had some connection with Judaism before becoming a Christian. Perhaps he was a God-fearer or synagogue adherent.

As J. D. G. Dunn made clear some time ago, for Paul the gift of the eschatological Spirit of God to believers in Christ is the first part of the redemption of the whole person. It is the Spirit who enables one to make a true confession that Jesus is the risen Lord (see 1 Cor. 12:3b) and it is also the Spirit who enables one to pray to God as *abba*. But it is not just that the Spirit in the believer's experience is the same Spirit as Jesus was anointed with at baptism (2 Cor. 1:21), though that is certainly true. In Paul's view the Holy Spirit is in some sense the Spirit of Christ, or put another way, of God's Son (cf. Gal. 4:6; Phil. 1:19; Rom. 8:9). This does not merely mean that it is the Spirit that Christ sent to believers, though that is true. The point is that the presence of God in the person of the Spirit replicates the spiritual life of Jesus in his followers' lives, conforming them to Jesus' image.[20] This includes enabling the believer to have the same sort of prayer life and intimate relationship with God as Jesus did. Indeed, the presence of this Spirit conforms one to the image of Jesus such that one becomes a son (or daughter) of God, on an analogy with Jesus being Son of God. Paul goes even further, suggesting that the presence of this Spirit not only prompts prayers like Jesus' prayers but enables one, as a son or daughter of God, to become fellow heirs with Jesus of the eschatological blessings (Rom. 8:17).

In Rom. 8:14-27 Paul elucidates what he means in some detail. What this passage suggests is that without the Holy Spirit in one's life, one would not be enabled to really pray to God as *abba,* or have one's prayer be an expression of the actual character of one's relationship with God. This text also intimates that the Spirit helps believers to pray beyond the level they would ordinarily be capable of praying, enabling the expressing of the unutterable desires and longings of the human heart to God in "sighs too deep for words." What this in turn seems to imply is that Paul takes for granted that this is the sort of prayer life Jesus himself had, and that *abba* is an expression of that deeper level of intimacy with God.

---

20. See J. D. G. Dunn, *Jesus and the Spirit* (Philadelphia: Westminster, 1975), pp. 317-19.

Several aspects of the Pauline treatment of the matter need to be elucidated. The passage begins with the declaration that it is those who are led by the Spirit of God who are children of God. In other words, just because one is a creature of God's making does not mean one is a child of God in the true sense of the phrase. This comports with what Paul goes on to say in v. 15, namely that the Spirit is the means by which a creature of God becomes an adopted son (or daughter) of God. It is because of this adoption, and not because of some Jewish tradition of calling God Father or of some ethnic link with pre-Christian Jews, that Christians are enabled to cry *"abba,* Father!" Notice the verb "cry" here, which suggests at the very least an earnest imploring of God, if not an ecstatic experience engendered by the Spirit. Indeed, v. 16 suggests that in a sense it is the Spirit who is doing the imploring of the Father, or at least the Spirit is providing the second witness or testifier, "bearing witness with our spirit." For Paul, the Spirit-prompted utterance of *"abba"* is in itself evidence that we are children of God. Only God's sons and daughters are able and enabled to cry *"abba."*

Yet lest his audience get too carried away, Paul emphasizes in vv. 18-27 that the Christian is in an already-and-not-yet situation. Already the believer has the Spirit and is enabled to pray as Jesus prayed, *"abba,* Father." But this ability is only the "first fruits of the Spirit" (v. 23),[21] and the truth is that we await the redemption of our bodies by means of resurrection. There is the cry of familial joy, *"abba,"* but there is also the groaning and longing for the redemption of the body (v. 23). But it is not merely our bodies that are not in a final state of bliss. Vv. 26-27 indicate that our minds are also not fully capable of articulating what we ought to be saying to God in prayer and so the Spirit intercedes and prays with and through the believer, with sighs too deep for words, a possible reference to glossolalia, but in any case a reference to a depth communication with God from the heart in a way that overcomes our inability to articulate such things. The Spirit is said to intercede for the saints according to the will of God (v. 27), which perhaps means the

21. The phrase, however, may mean that the Spirit is the first fruits, not merely that the Spirit has bestowed the first fruits of eschatological life in the believer.

Spirit conforms the believer's prayer to God's will since we do not adequately know how to pray.

In what is perhaps Paul's very earliest canonical letter, Galatians, written perhaps in A.D. 49, we have another reference to God as *abba* (Gal. 4:6-7). The context of this reference to *abba* is intriguing, for Paul in Gal. 4:4-5 is talking about how Jesus was sent by God as a Jew, born under the Law, to redeem those under the Law (i.e., Jews such as Paul himself), out from under that Law. This, says Paul, is the means by which we Jewish Christians have received adoption as sons (v. 5). The term *huiothesia* (adoption as sons) is an important one for Paul. It does not occur outside the Pauline corpus in the NT. Paul uses it with several different nuances (cf. Rom. 8:15, 23; 9:4; and Eph. 1:5). Paul indicates that adoption as sons belongs first and foremost to Jews, but it is "adoption" that he is referring to. Inclusion in the righteous remnant of Jews, which in Paul's view means Jewish Christians, is on the basis of grace, not natural inheritance or works (Rom. 10:5-6). In Paul's view God has imprisoned all under disobedience so he might have mercy on all by grace and through faith. Even Jews enter the new creation on the basis of grace and faith.

Paul then does not begin to speak of the condition of his Gentile converts in Galatia until Gal. 4:6. He is going to make clear that the Spirit of the Son has been sent into their lives not merely to give them the status of sons but to conform them spiritually to the character of the Son, which is characterized as involving the *abba* prayer language. Because the believer is truly a son, both objectively and subjectively he can pray (like the Son) to God as Father/*abba*. It is striking that here as in Rom. 8 we have exactly the same form of juxtaposition of Aramaic and Greek words for "father" as we found in Mk. 14:36 — literally "*abba*, the father" or simply "*abba*, Father." What this strongly suggests is that we have here not only a relic of the earliest Aramaic-speaking Jewish Christians' prayer language, though that is true, but the juxtaposition of the two terms suggests this had become common prayer language for non-Aramaic-speaking Christians, both Diaspora Jewish and Gentile ones, as well.

In the context of this letter, Paul is emphasizing that his Gentile converts in Galatia had been prompted by the Spirit to cry *"abba,"* just as Jewish Christians such as Paul had been earlier prompted to do. What greater proof could there be that they already had all the benefits of an intimate, loving relationship with God without having to submit to the Mosaic Law? Notice finally the use of the verb "cry," once more indicating that *abba* is an expression that comes from the depths of the believer's heart, perhaps suggesting a person full of heartfelt joy about his or her close relationship with the Father. So it is that the Spirit and what the Spirit prompts in the believer is both the evidence and the proof that the Galatian Gentiles are sons and no longer slaves.[22] Having carefully explored Paul's own use of the *abba* language, we may now go on to examine the broader use of Father language in the Pauline epistles.

There are some forty references to God as Father in Paul's letters, a number that is dwarfed by the some 500 times the word "God" *(theos)* appears in these same documents. Every one of the Pauline letters begins with some form of greeting or opening blessing that refers to God as either "our Father" (Rom. 1:7; 1 Cor. 1:3; 2 Cor. 1:2; Gal. 1:3-4; Eph. 1:2; Phil. 1:2; Col. 1:2; 2 Thess. 1:1), or "the Father" (Gal. 1:1; 1 Thess. 1:1; 1 Tim. 1:2; 2 Tim. 1:2; Titus 1:4), or more expansively "the Father of our Lord Jesus Christ" (2 Cor. 1:3; Eph. 1:3; Col. 1:3). Meye Thompson has rightly pointed out that the references to God as Father in Paul's letters tend to be found either in the opening remarks, or in benedictions, or in quotations of pre-set pieces such as the Christological hymn in Phil. 2. Notice for example that in the Pastorals and Philemon the term "Father" never occurs after the opening greeting and blessing.

In Galatians there are no references to God as Father after the letter opening except in the reference in Gal. 4:6 where it is coupled with the term *abba* (see above). Philippians refers to God as Father only in the closing benediction and at the end of the Christ hymn in Phil. 2. Romans, 1 Corinthians, and 2 Corinthians have three references or fewer to God as Father. What these statistics suggest is that Paul does not have a tendency to use the Father language outside of his source

---

22. See the fuller discussion in Ben Witherington III, *Grace in Galatia* (Edinburgh: T. & T. Clark, 1998), pp. 289-92.

material or outside of liturgical contexts (prayers, blessings, benedictions).[23] This in turn means that we cannot attribute the proliferation of Father language for God in early Christianity to the apostle to the Gentiles. Such language was already prevalent in the sources and worship contexts Paul was familiar with, and he simply echoed what he found there. This fact also strongly supports the suggestion that Paul's use of the *abba* language comes from his source material, ultimately from Jesus himself.

One of the interesting facets of Paul's use of Father language is that he almost never allows the term to stand alone. For example, when Paul refers to "our Father" it is always coupled with the term "God" — either "God our Father" or "Our God and Father." What this coupling suggests is that the term "Father" is not simply an equivalent for the term *theos* but a specification of the role God plays in relationship to believers — he is "our Father." This coupling also suggests that the term "Father" in and of itself was not sufficient to connote the idea of a divine being. It required further qualification by the context or by another term. But when we consider the confessional material in 1 Cor. 8:5-6 where Paul modifies the Shema ("Hear, O Israel, the Lord our God is one . . .") in a Christological way ("for us there is one God, the Father . . . and one Lord, Jesus Christ") we are reminded that Paul does not simply take over OT language for God. For example, he uses a phrase like "the Father of our Lord Jesus Christ"[24] to specify which God he is referring to (see Rom. 15:6; 2 Cor. 11:31), not a phrase like "the God of Abraham, Isaac, and Jacob."

As Meye Thompson stresses, Paul never refers to God as "my Father," unlike Jesus' practice.[25] Instead he stands with his fellow Christians in referring to God as "our Father." This is not an insignificant point. Paul does not see his own relationship to the Father as categorically different from that of his converts. Furthermore, it may be im-

---

23. For example, all references to God as "our Father" appear in some sort of prayer or benediction.

24. A phrase never found in the OT of course.

25. Meye Thompson, *The Promise of the Father*, pp. 120-21.

plied that while his own praying to God as *abba* replicates the practice of Jesus, he does not see his sonship as of the same order as the sonship of Jesus, who could speak of "my Father." One suspects that Paul distinguishes between adoptive sonship and Jesus' being the "natural" Son of God.

It is quite true that Paul, like several of the OT references to God as Father, stresses that he is a compassionate or merciful Father, who consoles those who are suffering (see 2 Cor. 1:3). But for the most part, Paul's usage of the Father language reflects the new eschatological situation that began with the coming, the death, and the resurrection of Jesus. For example, in Rom. 6:4 in a striking phrase Jesus is said to have been raised from the dead by the glory (i.e., powerful presence) of the Father. In 1 Cor. 15:24 we hear that after the second coming and after the Son has subdued the earth, he will turn the kingdom over to God the Father. The story that undergirds the references to the Fatherhood of God in Paul's letters is the story of Jesus, and the Father's relationship to him, not the story of Israel as a nation and God's relationship to Israel.[26] It is telling that God is not referred to as Father when Paul actually speaks at length about the heritage and future of Israel in Rom. 9–11. Nor is God's Fatherhood related to the forefatherhood of Abraham in Rom. 4.

In short, the Fatherhood of God is Christologically and eschatologically focused, not ecclesiologically focused in the Pauline corpus, except perhaps in Ephesians. But even in that homily the point of a text like Eph. 2:18 is surely that both Jews and Gentiles have access to the Father through the Son. It may be questioned too what the meaning of "all" is in Eph. 4:6. That verse is the culmination of a creedal fragment which is speaking specifically of the verities that are true for Christians. The one body, the one Spirit, the one hope, the one Lord, the one faith, the one baptism all refer to what Christians confess and what is true for and about them. Thus when we hear about the "one God and Father of all who is . . . in all" it seems hardly likely he is referring to the divine presence in all of creation or even in all creatures. It is far more likely

---

26. Pace Meye Thompson, *The Promise of the Father,* p. 132.

the reference is to God who is specifically the Father of believers and dwells in them.

We have seen in Paul's use of Father language further justification for thinking that the earliest followers of Jesus used the language as they did because of the way Jesus had used the language, and because of what they believed to be true about Jesus' relationship to the Father. They believed that they had become adopted sons of God because of the Son of God, and they had access to the Father through the Son. Indeed, they believed that in an analogous fashion the Spirit replicated the prayer life of the Son in them. They also believed that they did not have independent access to the Father, but rather had that access through the Son and by means of the Spirit. By that means they had come to have an intimate relationship with God, whether they were Jews or Gentiles.

The story of the Father is linked eschatologically and soteriologically to the work of redemption that happens exclusively through the Son. It is through him that believers are linked to the Father, and they view the Father through the eyes and relationship of the Son to him.

Yet there is a difference. Though both Jesus and his followers cry "*abba*, Father," the former does so as the begotten Son, the latter do so as the adoptive sons. The former does so as the redeemer, the latter do so as the redeemed. Thus while there is analogous intimacy between the Father and the Son and the Father and the sons, it is not identical intimacy because the respective relationships are not identical in every respect. We must turn now to examine the Father language found in the Synoptic Gospels and their sources (Mark, Q, M, and L).[27]

III. The Father in the Synoptics

In her treatment of the Synoptic Gospels Meye Thompson argues that "what emerges as distinctive in all the Gospels is the singling out of the

---

27. Q refers to the material Matthew and Luke share in common which is not found in Mark. M refers to uniquely Matthean material. L refers to uniquely Lukan material.

relationship of Jesus to the Father *as an exceptional instance of the Father/Son relationship.*"[28] But would it not be better to speak of that relationship as unique rather than merely exceptional? Instead of trying to fit Jesus' relationship into some earlier or larger paradigm, would it not be better to say that Jesus' relationship becomes the paradigm of the relationship of his followers to the Father in certain limited but real ways? Is it really true as, Meye Thompson suggests, that the references to God as Father of believers is simply being carried over from early Judaism and is not basically grounded in Jesus' own usage and experience of God?[29] We must explore the data and see what emerges.

There are only four references to God as Father in the earliest Gospel, Mark, one of which is the garden of Gethsemane incidence that we have already treated.[30] There is in addition the reference to the Son of Man coming in the Father's glory at Mk. 8:38. We have seen the theme of the glory of the Father when we considered the Pauline material. Jesus' exaltation according to Phil. 2 did not subtract from God the Father's glory but added to it, and in a striking phrase in Rom. 6:4 Jesus was raised by the glory of the Father. What Mk. 8:38 is suggesting is that the Son of Man will come imbued with the divine power and imprimatur, but more importantly will come embodying the divine presence associated with the Father. There is a possibility, however, of reading Mk. 8:38 in a non-traditional manner. The word *angelloi* need not be translated "angels"; it can refer to human messengers. Furthermore, the verb "comes" can simply refer to an appearing. This leads to the suggestion that Mk. 8:38 and 9:1 are both referring to the transfiguration story recorded in Mk. 9:2-8, where Jesus appeared radiant with Moses and Elijah, the two great messengers and holy men of the OT. In either case, the text indicates that the Son of Man will have properties that only properly belong to God the Father. This is part of Mark's portrayal of Jesus as divine.

A third text is found in Mk. 11:25 where the Father in heaven is said to forgive our trespasses, provided we forgive our fellow humans their

28. Meye Thompson, *The Promise of the Father,* p. 88, italics mine.
29. Meye Thompson, *The Promise of the Father,* p. 89.
30. See above, pp. 22-25.

trespasses. If Mk. 8:38 stresses the glory of the Father, this text stresses a frequent theme found in the teachings of Jesus, namely the compassion and forgiving nature of the Father. This idea of course has some precedent in OT texts such as Hos. 11:8-9. Here, however, it is linked to human forgiveness, as is the case in the Lord's Prayer as well. The vertical relationship with God is affected by one's horizontal relationship with fellow human beings, particularly believers, so far as the matter of forgiveness is concerned. This appears to strike a new note in the discussion of the way the Father operates, which does not really find precedent in the OT or in the literature of early Judaism.[31]

A fourth text is Mk. 13:32, which indicates that there is some knowledge only the Father has, in this case the knowledge of the timing of the second coming. Here then we see a distinction between the Father and the Son in knowledge, at least so long as the Son had an earthly ministry. To this of course we may add Mk. 14:36, which indicates that the Father's will is the ultimate arbiter of human destiny, including Jesus'. This comports nicely with what we find in other Markan texts such as Mk. 10:27, which stresses that all things are possible for God. Overall, the portrait of the Father in Mark is of an omniscient, omnipotent, but also omni-benevolent deity, who has a special relationship with the Son. This relationship involves shared glory, shared knowledge to some extent, shared power, and a common commitment to the will of God. The Father is one to whom Jesus could turn in his darkest hour and be heard, all the while having his own will conformed to the will of the Father. Jesus is the Beloved Son as the baptismal and transfiguration stories make apparent (Mk. 1:11; 9:7), which makes it all the more striking that the Father's will is for him to die on a cross as a ransom for many.[32]

---

31. Targum I on Lev. 22:28 does indeed read "My people, children of Israel, as our Father is merciful in heaven, so you shall be merciful on earth" (and cf. Targum on Is. 63:16 and 64:8). These texts, however, are notoriously difficult to date, and probably come from after the time of Jesus, perhaps after the NT era. In other words, they may well reflect the influence in the other direction of Jesus' and early Christian teaching on Jewish teaching, which we know did happen in other cases, for example in speculation about the Suffering Servant of Is. 53.

32. On Mark's portrait of the Son see pp. 80-83 below.

Like Mark, Luke does not really use the term "Father" that frequently for God. It is found only seventeen times in our longest Gospel, and only three more times in Acts (1:4, 7; 2:33). One could not say it is a major redactional agenda of Luke to add references to the Father to his source material. By comparison we find some 122 times in Luke's Gospel and 168 times in Acts where *theos* is used for God. As Meye Thompson stresses, *all* references to God as Father in Luke-Acts are in Jesus' own speech with one exception — the last reference to the Father in Acts 2:33.[33] The proper conclusion to be drawn from this is that Luke not only sees such speech as characteristic of Jesus, but indeed as distinctive of his discourse, as opposed even to that of some of his followers. Only the leader of the Twelve, Peter, is portrayed as using the Father language as Jesus did, and only after Easter and after the Holy Spirit has been poured out. No text portrays any disciple using such language before Easter, though of course Jesus instructs his disciples to pray this way at Lk. 11:2. This comports well with the stress in Lk. 10:22 that no one knows the Father except the Son.

Jesus himself in Luke-Acts refers to God as "my Father" and when speaking to the disciples as "your Father," but he does not refer to "our Father." Six of the seventeen passages in Luke's Gospel that refer to God as Father do not derive from Mark or Q but rather are unique to his Gospel (Lk. 2:49; 12:32; 22:29; 23:34; 24:49). A further nine instances come from Luke's Q source (Lk. 6:36; 10:21-22; 11:2; 11:13; 12:30). Luke sometimes simply uses the phrase "the Father," as in Lk. 11:2, but he can also use the more elaborate "the heavenly Father" (11:13).[34]

Our discussion of Luke's use of Father language for God must begin with the birth narrative. Here, as Meye Thompson has rightly stressed, three different figures are called Father — David (1:32), Joseph (2:33, 48), and God.[35] But the first reference to Father on Jesus' lips at Lk. 2:49 stands as something of a correction. God is Jesus' true Father (cf. the genealogy in Lk. 3:38), and he must be in his heavenly Father's

---

33. Meye Thompson, *The Promise of the Father,* p. 93.

34. This sort of phrase is found only once in Mark — Mk. 11:25.

35. Meye Thompson, *The Promise of the Father,* p. 94.

house doing his will. Here then we have a reference to God having a house on earth, namely the Temple, and Jesus having a special relationship to the Father such that he must be at work in his house, like a good son (cf. Lk. 15:29).

Lk. 6:36 stresses the mercy of the Father and urges disciples to emulate such behavior. If Lk. 23:34 is originally part of Luke's Gospel it also sounds this theme. Jesus asks the Father to forgive those who are crucifying him for they do not know what they are doing.[36] The Q material in Lk. 10:21-22 has Jesus referring to God as "my Father," and here the Father is pictured as the all-knowing One who has revealed certain crucial truths only to a certain few. The Father is called in prayer at 10:21a "the Lord of heaven and earth," and he is said to have a gracious will in 10:21b. The end of v. 22 makes clear that true knowledge of the Father is only dispensed by the Son to anyone he chooses.

In the Lukan form of the Lord's Prayer, which he derived from his Q source (Lk. 11:2-4), God is simply called Father and said to have a Dominion and a will. He is the one who dispenses daily bread and forgives debts, and he is the one who could bring the believer to the point of trial (just as he was to do with Jesus at the close of his ministry). At Lk. 12:30 the Father is the one said again to provide for the disciples' material needs. Back at 11:13 God is called the heavenly Father and is said to give good gifts, in particular the gift of the Holy Spirit to those who ask him for it. Of course in the Lukan scheme of things this is the ultimate eschatological gift of God that was to enable the disciples to be a church, to be missionaries, and to address God as Father — to mention but a few of the benefits of the bestowal of the Spirit.

At Lk. 12:30-32 Jesus encourages his followers by stressing the benevolent will of the Father — it is his desire and good pleasure to give the Dominion to them. He knows the disciples' material needs, and because he is "your Father" he desires to give them both the Dominion and these additional things as well. It is interesting that in the Lukan telling

36. We agree with J. B. Green, *The Gospel of Luke* (Grand Rapids: Eerdmans, 1997), p. 817, that it is likely original to Luke's Gospel. It nicely comports with the theme of ignorance about this matter that appears for instance in Acts 3:17.

of things Jesus actually tells his disciples at the last supper "I confer on you, just as my Father has conferred on me, a Dominion" (Lk. 22:29).[37]

After Easter we have the saying of Jesus about the Holy Spirit at Lk. 24:49. Here Jesus is said to be the sender of what the Father had all along promised. This builds on what was said at 11:13 about the gift of the Holy Spirit. This leads quite naturally to Acts 1:4 where Jesus commands the disciples to stay in Jerusalem and receive the promise of the Father (i.e., the Holy Spirit). At Acts 1:7-8 we have the interesting contrast between what the disciples do not get from God and what they do. It is not for them to receive the knowledge of the eschatological timing of things that the Father has set by his own authority, but it is for them to receive the Holy Spirit as promised and be witnesses throughout the earth. The image of the Father as in control of time and timing, and as one who empowers believers to spread the Good News, is clear here.

Perhaps the most familiar Lukan text that seems to deal with God as Father is the parable of the prodigal son, found in Lk. 15:11-32. The story is indeed about a compassionate Father who welcomes back the repentant lost son. As Meye Thompson stresses, understanding Jewish treatments of the matter of inheritance is important in this parable. The prodigal takes and squanders his inheritance prematurely, thereby forfeiting even his status as a son. But the prodigal recognizes what he has done and repents of it.[38] But as Meye Thompson stresses, the father in the parable is not merely a forgiving father but a reconciling father who restores the son's place in the family as a son and seeks to reconcile the elder and younger sons.

The overall portrait of the Father in Luke-Acts is of an extremely compassionate, forgiving and giving (both material and spiritual blessings) God. But the fact that only Jesus speaks of God as Father during his ministry, and only Jesus is said to truly know the Father and can both call

37. Meye Thompson, *The Promise of the Father,* p. 95, suggests we see this as a passing on of inheritance. However, Jesus has not inherited the Dominion, for the Father has not died, unless one wishes to see this as another case like that in the parable of the prodigal son in Lk. 15 where the inheritance is dispensed out of due season, before the father died.

38. Meye Thompson, *The Promise of the Father,* pp. 101-2.

him "my Father" and reveal him, shows that Luke believes Jesus had a distinctive, indeed unique and unprecedented relationship with the Father. Once the promise of the Father, namely the Spirit, is bestowed, the disciples can in a derivative sense speak of God as Father. The fact that they only once do so, and in that case it is only Peter, the spokesman of the Twelve, doing it, merely accentuates the Lukan stress on the uniqueness of Jesus' relationship to his Father. This Father/Son relationship is in various ways not a relationship shared by Israel earlier with God, nor afterwards is this relationship simply transferable in toto to Jesus' disciples. Only the presence of the Spirit in the believer's life enables an approximation of such an intimate relationship.

When one turns to the Matthean portrait of the Father one is immediately struck by the abundance of references to the Father in contrast to what we find in Mark or Luke-Acts. Matthew in fact uses Father language for God more than Mark and Luke together. More often than not "Father" is prefaced by some sort of possessive ("my" or "your") in Matthew's Gospel (cf., e.g., Lk. 22:42 to Mt. 26:39). Especially telling is a comparison with Luke. Luke has "my Father" four times, Matthew fourteen times, while Luke has "your Father" three times, Matthew fifteen times. Luke's Gospel, in terms of numbers of Greek words and lines, is in fact a bit longer than Matthew's.

Meye Thompson makes a telling comparison of Matthew's and Luke's use of Q and Mark in relevant passages with the following results: (1) in Mt. 6:26 where the First Evangelist has "your heavenly Father" in the parallel in Lk. 12:24 we simply find "God"; (2) in Mt. 10:20 where Matthew has "the Spirit of your Father," Luke simply has "Holy Spirit" (Lk. 12:12); (3) Mk. 3:35 and Lk. 8:21 both have "God" when speaking of "whoever does the will *of God* is my brother . . ." but Matthew has "the will *of my Father in heaven* . . ." (Mt. 12:50); (4) while Mk. 14:25 and Lk. 22:19 both refer to "the kingdom of God," Mt. 26:29 refers to "my Father's kingdom."[39] S. Barton is surely right that for "Matthew, God's presence is experienced as fatherly."[40]

---

39. Meye Thompson, *The Promise of the Father,* p. 106.
40. S. C. Barton, *The Spirituality of the Gospels* (London: SPCK, 1992), p. 12.

It is significant that not only do we find more use of the phrase "heavenly Father" in Matthew than in the other Synoptics combined, but we also find a decided preference for the phrase "kingdom of heaven" rather than "kingdom of God" in Matthew. In this phrase we are dealing with the use of "heaven" as a Jewish circumlocution for God. It is telling then that Matthew has no hesitation to speak of "the Father," but he is more reticent to use the term "God." This may well reflect the early instincts of Jewish Christians who had been instructed by Jesus to speak of and pray to the Father, but who still retained their Jewish reluctance about saying the divine name, or an equivalent like the word *theos.* This also bears witness to the fact that "Father" was not seen as a proper name for God. Rather it was a term describing a very personal relationship.

Lest we think that the phrase "heavenly Father" describes God's character, texts like Mt. 12:50 and 18:14 show that the author can equally well use the phrase "Father in heaven." Heaven is the locale of the Father. Meye Thompson is right that Matthew has a special stress on the will of the Father and uses that phrase rather than "the will of God" (cf. Mt. 6:10; 11:25; 12:50; 26:39, 42 to 21:31). Only Matthew has the following verse: "And call no one your father on earth, for you have one Father — the one in heaven" (Mt. 23:9). This text is famously the main one used by E. Schüssler-Fiorenza to argue that Jesus stressed the Fatherhood of God to undermine the patriarchal emphasis on human fathers (and teachers called father or *abba*) and their power and authority.[41] There seems to be some real substance to this argument, not least because Jesus sets up the family of faith as his own and his followers'

41. E. Schüssler-Fiorenza, *In Memory of Her* (New York: Crossroad, 1983), pp. 150-51: "The new kinship of equals does not admit of 'fathers' thereby rejecting the patriarchal power and esteem invested in them. . . . The 'father' God is invoked here, however, not to justify patriarchal structures and relationships in the community of disciples but precisely to reject all such claims, powers, and structures. . . . The address 'father' used by Jesus and his disciples has caused many Christian feminists great scandal because the church has not obeyed the command of Jesus 'to call no one father,' for you have 'one father' and because it has resulted in legitimizing ecclesial and societal patriarchy with the 'father' name of God, thereby using the name of God in vain."

primary family. This text also suggests not only that human fatherhood is not being taken as the model of what God's Fatherhood amounts to, but also God's Fatherhood is seen as unique and all-encompassing, and so not a paradigm for fathers in particular. All are to be merciful as the heavenly Father is merciful.

Yet one can have hierarchy among disciples without it being specifically grounded in patriarchy. Matthew's Gospel not only recognizes the absolute hierarchy of believers being dependent on and subservient to God but also, in Mt. 16:17-20, refers to Peter being given a role of authority over believers. But in the end, it must not be forgotten that Mt. 23:8-10 and its discussion about fathers is set in a context of a discussion about teachers, and as Meye Thompson says, the real thrust of the prohibition is making sure no merely human instructor or teacher is put in the place of the real Instructor Jesus, and of the real Father, God.[42]

Mt. 6:25-32 is an important text, for it tells us something of Matthew's conception of the Father. Notice how the Father's provision for his people is seen as analogous to his care and provision for other creatures. Barton is quite right that Matthew sees God's fatherly work involving his being the creator and sustainer of the world, as well as the creator and sustainer of human beings, particularly believers.[43] This is an important point, for it makes clear that unlike human fathers, who are not the creators of the material world or of non-human creatures, God's Fatherhood encompasses all he has made and begotten. In other words, the roles of human fathers in a patriarchal system are not simply being projected onto God.

Human actions such as good works amount to a human approximation of the benevolence of God, and may cause people to give glory to the Father (Mt. 5:16) who has prompted and enabled such human actions. Yet again, such actions are only pale shadows or imitations of the divine actions of God as Father. Being a child of the Father means loving in analogous manner to the way that the Father loves (5:45). So great is the Father's compassion and love that it is not his desire or will

---

42. Meye Thompson, *The Promise of the Father,* pp. 108-9.
43. Barton, *The Spirituality of the Gospels,* p. 12.

that "one of these little ones [i.e., younger or weaker disciples] should be lost" (18:11-14). This sort of selfless loving attitude and action is what is being referred to when the author urges believers to be perfect as the heavenly Father is perfect (5:48). Human actions are also said to be of consequence not only in terms of witness or imitation of the Father, but in the way they affect one's eternal destiny. Mt. 7:21 is quite clear that it is the one who does the will of the Father, not merely the one who cries "Lord, Lord," who will enter the Dominion of God. This comports with the parable of the sheep and goats in Mt. 25:31-46, where we learn that only the sheep will be told "come, you blessed of my Father, inherit the Dominion prepared for you from the foundation of the world," and the basis of the distinction between sheep and goats is said to be the charitable deeds to the stranger, naked, and poor that the "sheep" performed (and so ministered to Jesus the shepherd indirectly). It is also doing the will of the Father that demonstrates who are Jesus' kinfolk — mothers, brothers, sisters (Mt. 12:50).[44]

None of the analogies in Matthew between the disciple's character and conduct and that of Jesus, or even the analogies between the character and conduct of the disciple and that of the Father, should be allowed to obscure the fact that "Matthew still retains the singularity of Jesus' address to God as 'my Father' and his admonitions to his disciples regarding obedience to 'your Father.' Clearly there is a distinction between the way Jesus addresses the Father and the way in which the disciples do. Matthew's manifest predilection for the formulation 'my Father' reflects his understanding of the distinctive character of Jesus' Sonship and the relationship of the Father and the Son."[45] This is a correct observation, but it needs to be stressed that we also saw this in the

---

44. Notice that Jesus does not speak of someone being his "father" if he does the will of the Father. This is because of Jesus' view about the exclusive role that the heavenly Father plays in his life, and to judge from Mt. 23:9, in the lives of his disciples as well.

45. Meye Thompson, *The Promise of the Father*, p. 111. This is correct and precisely why citing a saying like Jer. 3:19 as a parallel is not very apt, for there God is hoping that all true Israelites would call him "my Father" (even though, in the event, they have not done so, but rather have been unfaithful).

Pauline material, in the material in Mark, and even in the material that goes back to the historical Jesus. It is just that Matthew highlights this Christological distinctiveness more, as does the Fourth Evangelist.

We may begin to note in Matthew a pattern emerging — the higher the Christology in a NT document, the more likely there is to be a strong emphasis on the Father and his distinctive roles and relationships with Jesus and others (not merely a greater frequency of Father language). The more focus on the Son, the more focus on the Father as well, to make clear the distinctive relationship the Son has with the Father. The Father is "the Father of our Lord Jesus Christ," and this is one of the main things that distinguishes this Father from other deities (or emperors) that might be called Father. Soteriologically as well, the more emphasis on Jesus as the means of salvation, the more the emphasis on human beings' relationships with the Father going through the Son. One comes to the Father of Jesus through Jesus. This comports with the suggestion that the Father is seen through the eyes of the Son in the NT, as well as related to by means of one's relationship with Jesus. All such discussions are grounded in the intimate relationship between the Son and the Father referred to in the Q saying that Matthew repeats, about only the Father knowing the Son and vice versa.

It is true to say that as the Synoptic writers portray things, "God's Fatherhood serves not as a model for the behavior of a human father, nor does it in some way give shape to the nuclear family. Rather, God's Fatherhood serves as the model for the life of the faithful community together. All are called to reflect God's mercy and love. No one reflects God's fatherhood more or less by virtue of status, birth, gender, or class. All are to call on God, and only on God, as Father, and together all are family, brothers and sisters, children of God."[46] All of this is true, but it must not be allowed to lessen a proper stress on the fact that all such talk is grounded in the reality of the relationship disciples must have with Jesus to be and do such things, and in turn is grounded in Jesus' own unique relationship with the Father. The relationship of the community to the Father goes through the relationship they have with

---

46. Meye Thompson, *The Promise of the Father,* p. 115.

the Son, and it is dependent on the Son's own relationship with the Father as a source and model of such relating to the Father. This point is made even more explicitly and clearly in the Fourth Gospel.

IV. The Father of the Word — the Fourth Gospel

When we reach the Fourth Gospel, we reach the apex of the use of Father language for God in the Gospels. In fact, here for the first time the term "Father" is found more frequently than even the term *theos* itself. About 120 times John refers to God as Father, and 108 times he simply uses the term "God" *(theos),* but the terms are not just interchangeable. For example, there is a stress on it being the Father who sends the Son, and the Father's will that the Son does.[47] It is crucial to bear in mind that the Christological orientation and tone of this document is set right at the outset in the Logos hymn that makes up the Prologue. This Gospel will be about the pre-existent Word who took on flesh and dwelled for a time with human beings. In Jn. 1:14-18, where the subject of the incarnation is first broached, we hear for the first time about the Father. The glory of the only *(monogenes)* Son from the Father is what was seen by the audience. While the term *monogenes* could refer to the unique (only one of its kind) Son, it probably does convey the sense of begetting, in which case the translation "only begotten Son" would be appropriate. The point is that this Son comes directly from the Father who is the begetter. Jesus is not an adopted Son of God. The Son proceeds from the Father as like produces or begets like. He was not created as something or someone inherently distinct from the being of the Father. This affirmation stands in a context where we are told that human beings become the children of God by receiving the Word and believing in his name and being born of God (1:12-13). There is thus a clear distinction made between the only "natural" or begotten Son, and those who become chil-

---

47. Meye Thompson, *The Promise of the Father,* p. 134.

48. See Ben Witherington III, *John's Wisdom* (Louisville: Westminster/John Knox, 1995), pp. 54-55.

dren of God by belief and response to the Word.[48] It is quite true to say that John emphasizes more than the other Gospels the unique relationship of the Son to the Father, but this is more of a difference in degree of emphasis than a difference in kind of emphasis.

As was the case with the Synoptics, the references to God as Father in the Fourth Gospel come almost solely on the lips of Jesus himself. Indeed, Jesus is the only one who addresses God as Father in this Gospel.[49] As in the other Gospels there is the distinctive "my Father" found on the lips of Jesus (about two dozen times), as well as "the Father" (more than 85 times) and simply "Father" or "holy Father" (eight of the former, one of the latter), but in John we also have the different stress on "the Father who sent me."

Jesus is seen most clearly in this Gospel as the agent or apostle of God sent on a mission from heaven to earth (see 8:26-27). As a sent one the Son only speaks and acts on the authority of the Father, but at the same time the Father has only authorized his only Son to do the things that we see Jesus doing in this Gospel. The Twelve fade almost entirely out of view in the Gospel, so clear is the biographical focus on the words and deeds of the Son. This perhaps explains why we only have "your Father" spoken to the disciples once, and even in this case it is after Easter (20:17). Jesus neither uses the phrase "our Father" in this Gospel, nor does he teach the disciples to pray this way in John. "What is particularly telling in the depiction of God as Father is the way in which God's actions as Father are focused on Jesus himself. It is Jesus who speaks of, and addresses, God as Father. Jesus speaks but rarely even to his disciples of God as their father, and then only after the resurrection. In short, according to [this] Gospel it is the prerogative of Jesus to address God as Father and speak of God in these terms."[50]

In this Gospel, the theological implications of Jesus' use of Father language are made clear at various junctures. For instance, in Jn. 5:17-18 when Jesus says "My Father is still working, and I also am working," we

49. There are some editorial examples of the use of "Father" such as in Jn. 5:18, which shows that the usage also reflects what was going on in the Fourth Evangelist's day.

50. Meye Thompson, *The Promise of the Father,* p. 134.

are told that some Jews sought to kill him in part because "he was calling God his own Father, thereby making himself equal to God." Jesus, according to the Fourth Evangelist, was definitely claiming some sort of distinctive status and relationship with the Father. This manifests itself in several ways. For example, when some Jews argue with Jesus and claim God as their Father, Jesus disputes this claim (8:41-42). Only Jesus and his disciples are expected to be able to use such intimate language of God.

It cannot be overemphasized how much John stresses the unity and love and intimacy between the Father and the Son. For example, the mutual affection between the Father and the Son comes up at various points (Jn. 3:35; 5:20; 10:17), but only once is it said that God loved the world (3:16), or that the Father loves the disciples (16:27). Notice that it is the term "God" which is used when talking about the love of the world, whereas it is the term "Father" which is used when the text refers to the love of the disciples. The family relationship does not exist between God and the world, even though he loves the world. Even to some antagonistic Jews Jesus says "If God were your Father, you would love me, for I came from God . . ." (8:42). According to this Gospel, people must first become children of God through faith, before God is truly their Father, and that entails first also having a relationship with Jesus.[51] The Son has been bequeathed life from the Father, and he is the one who bestows it and the relationship with God it involves on others (5:25-26). He indeed is the way, the truth, and the life in soteriological matters. If you know the Son, you also know the Father, for he is the very image of the Father, only saying and doing what the Father would say and do (8:19). "The 'kinship' of God and Jesus as Father and Son becomes the basis for a number of claims made for Jesus. These claims include his authority to judge, to give life, to mediate knowledge of the Father and to reveal him, to do the work and will of the Father, and therefore to receive honor, as even the Father does."[52] Jesus has the Fa-

---

51. It is not going too far then to say that in John "There is no Father without the Son. Father is not something that God is apart from relationship to the Son" (Meye Thompson, *The Promise of the Father,* p. 137).

52. Rightly, Meye Thompson, *The Promise of the Father,* pp. 135-36.

ther's presence always with him (8:29a), he has been instructed by the Father and so instructs others (Jn. 8:28), and all that Jesus does pleases the Father (8:29b). Indeed, the Father testifies on behalf of Jesus (8:18) and even glorifies Jesus (8:54) and gives all things into Jesus' hands (3:35), and Jesus honors his Father in all he says and does (8:49) and keeps the Father's word (8:55).

The dialogue that we find in Jn. 8:31-59 between Jesus and some Jews who had begun to believe in him is very revealing. The argument of these Jews is that they have Abraham as their father; they are descendants of Abraham and therefore they don't need to be liberated from some sort of bondage or slavery. But a natural linkage to the fatherhood of Abraham is not sufficient to save a person. Indeed, as it turns out, Jesus is going to claim that they have neither God nor Abraham as their true father. The father whose image they bear and whose actions they emulate and manifest is the Devil (8:44).

These Jews press the matter and ask Jesus if he is greater than their father Abraham so that he can claim his disciples will never see death, when even Abraham died (8:52-53). Jesus then makes the astounding claim that he existed before Abraham (8:58), a claim that leads to an attempted stoning. The fatherhood of Abraham is not seen as a bad thing, but what Jesus claims is that if they really knew their Jewish heritage and were true descendants of Abraham, like Abraham, they would welcome Jesus and his "day." The fact that they do not do so shows they are not true descendants of Abraham. In any case the really crucial thing is whether one is a child of the Father through discipleship to Jesus, not whether one is a biological descendant of Abraham. The issue of paternity comes up in various ways in this passage, even to the extent of questioning Jesus' natural paternity (8:41 seems to imply Jesus' is illegitimate, while that of his dialogue partners is not). But again the paternity that matters is the Fatherhood of God. In a sense, we have here the Johannine version of the Q theme about calling no one Father but God.

As Meye Thompson shows, the phrase "the living God" is not uncommon in the OT (cf. Deut. 5:26; 1 Sam. 17:26, 36; 2 Kings 19:4, 16; Jer. 23:36; as opposed to dead idols) and in the NT (cf. Mt. 16:26; 26:63;

Acts 14:15; Rom. 9:26; 2 Cor. 3:3; 6:16; 1 Thess. 1:9; 3:15; 1 Tim. 4:10; Heb. 3:12; 9:14; 10:31; 12:22).[53] Such texts could easily be further illuminated by other kinds of similar references from non-canonical early Jewish texts.[54] Here we note that John does not use the phrase "the living God" but instead "the living Father." This interesting and telling phrase indicates that "as the eternally existent, living God, God alone is the source of all life. . . . The affirmation that God is Father cannot be separated from the affirmation that God is the source of life, nor from the conviction that the life of the Father has been given to, and comes to human beings through, the Son."[55] The Father has life in himself and has granted the Son the same privilege (5:25-26), another clear indication of the divinity of the Son as portrayed in this Gospel.[56] This is no doubt one of the reasons why Jesus can say "I and the Father are one" (10:30), for Jesus is able to do the same work that the Father can do. He has the life within himself, so he can even say he *is* the Resurrection and the Life, not merely that he gives them. Only in Jesus'

53. Meye Thompson, *The Promise of the Father,* p. 139.

54. One could add texts from early Judaism as well. 4Q504; Joseph and Aseneth 8:4; and note that Philo says that God is the Father of all things because he begat them (*Cher.* 49).

55. Meye Thompson, *The Promise of the Father,* p. 141.

56. This brings up a crucial point in the debate about the use of Father language for God. Technically speaking only fathers are begetters, only mothers conceivers of life. If indeed the begetting power of God, when it comes to life, is seen as one of the most fundamental functions of God who has life in himself, then it is not only appropriate to call God Father, it is necessary to do so. In other words, there is being predicated of God in this case what we as humans recognize as an exclusively male function. One could focus this discussion more particularly and point out that according to the birth narratives God is the Father who generated the human nature of Jesus, and Mary the mother who conceived him. This in turn would seem to imply that to call God Mother would not send the same message at all as to call God Father. God as Mother would be the recipient of the source of life and the conceiver of life.

Thus while God is not a male, he is clearly portrayed in Scripture as assuming male-specific functions. It could also be argued that the reason Jesus could never call God Mother was precisely because God had not been that for him or played that role in relationship to him; rather Mary had. God had played the role of Father, "begetting" the Son, both eternally and temporally.

case he has been given the eschatological task of calling the dead to life (Jn. 5:25-26), creating humans from scratch. It follows from this that those who take Jesus within themselves will have everlasting life (Jn. 6:53-57). The living Father has sent the living Son who comes to indwell the believers so they might have life within them, life abundant and everlasting as John 6 suggests. There is then a sense in which it is true to say that God's Fatherhood, insofar as new life is concerned, is carried out through the Son.[57] More could be said along these lines, but this is sufficient to make clear that it is correct to say that the higher the Christological reflection, the more likely the proliferation of Father language for God, precisely because it is the Father-Son duo in a high Christology that must be linked and indeed explained to some degree. The more one says about the Son, the more one needs to explain about the Father, lest one think the Father has been eclipsed or supplanted or has faded from the scene.

V. The Father in the General Epistles and in the Rest of the Johannine Corpus

Hebrews

Hebrews is a large document with thirteen chapters, and in some ways could be said to be the most thoroughly Jewish and Old Testamental of all the NT documents, with the possible exceptions of Matthew and Revelation. It is perhaps not surprising then that there are precious few references to God as Father in this document, for that is rarely terminology found for God in the OT.[58] Indeed, there is as much use of a circumlocution for God like "the Majesty" or "the Majesty on High" (cf. 1:3 to 8:1) as there is of Father language.

At Heb. 1:5 we do have a quotation of one of the few OT texts that refers to God as Father — 2 Sam. 7:14 (cf. 1 Chron. 17:13). Heb. 1:5 is

---

57. See Meye Thompson, *The Promise of the Father*, p. 145.
58. See pp. 1-19 above.

prefaced by a quote of Ps. 2:7 where a reference to the begetting of the Son (an adoption formula applied to the king on coronation day) is mentioned. Notice that what is said is that God will be as a Father to the Son, and vice versa. In other words, what is being referred to is how God will relate to Jesus. It is not so much a commentary on the divine nature.

In Hebrews 2 we have one striking passage of relevance to our discussion. Heb. 2:10-12 refers to the fact that God is the one through whom and by whom all things exist. Then there is an indirect mention of Christ, as the pioneer of the believers' salvation, being perfected through sufferings. Then the author says, "For the one who sanctifies [i.e., Christ] and those who are sanctified [i.e., believers] are all of the One. For this reason he [Jesus] is not ashamed to call them brothers." There is no direct use of the Father language here, although various translations add the term at 2:11 to explain who the One is (see the NRSV), but the concept is present here, and what is interesting is that Jesus and believers are placed on the same plane — all are "of the One." In other words, God is the source of all extant beings. More specifically he is their Father in the sense of being their source of life. This is why Jesus can refer to believers as family — they share the same heavenly Parent. There is no distinction made between Jesus' relationship with the One and that of believers at this juncture, but then our author tends to identify Christ as the believers' forerunner in various regards (see Heb. 12:2). The author could very well have used the phrase "Father of spirits" to describe God here, as we shall now see that he does in Heb. 12.

Striking by its absence is any reference to God as Father in the hall of faith chapter, where OT events are recounted. This suggests that the author is not simply following OT practices in regard to calling God Father, but derives this language for God from elsewhere, namely Christian practice. In Heb. 12:7-11 we have an interesting brief discourse on the Father-son relationship between God and believers. Here the reference is to divine discipline or chastening through trials. Disciplining, says the author, proves one is a member of the family, and that one has a Father who cares about one's life and moral character. The disciplining is said to lead to our sharing God's holiness and righteousness.

There is a plea to be subject to the Father of spirits (12:9). This is an atypical way of referring to the Father in the NT, and perhaps it suggests God's supervision of the human spirit.

James

In the homily attributed to James we have three references to God as Father. The first is not found at the beginning of the document but rather at 1:17 where we find the unique phrase "the Father of Lights," an apparent reference to the Father dwelling in the realm of eternal light (i.e., in heaven), but it could equally well be a reference to God being light, for the author goes on to say there is no shadow of turning in him. The Father is said to be the one who sends down from heaven every good and perfect gift or blessing that his audience receives. The image is of the perfect Father who is supremely generous to his children. At James 1:27 we have a reference to God the Father, who is said to be concerned with the quality of our religion and in particular is concerned for the appropriate treatment of orphans and widows. At James 3:9 we have a reference to blessing "the Lord and Father." While this could be a reference to one person, elsewhere in James the Lord is always the Lord Jesus Christ (see, e.g., 2:1; 5:7), and so it likely refers to the adoration of both the Father and of the Lord Jesus. Here verbal adoration is indicated. While there is not a lot of theological discourse in this document, this last reference bears witness to the nature of early Christian piety, which involved praying to and worshiping and giving thanks not only to the Father but also to the Son.

1 Peter

Three times in 1 Peter the term "Father" is applied to God, all three examples being in the first chapter. Believers are said in the opening greeting to have been chosen and destined by God the Father (1:2). The image is of an active God working out his plan for his people in human history. At 1:3 we have the important phrase "the God and Father of our Lord Jesus Christ," highlighting the unique relationship the Son has with the Father, and perhaps the sense that believers are closer to the Son (he is "our Lord," whereas God is more formally "the Father"). The phrase also seems to imply that the Father is Jesus' God. Especially important is the reference in 1:17 that refers to "invoking as Father the one who judges all people impartially." This reference confirms that Christians were indeed praying to God as Father when this letter was written. The Father is characterized as the impartial judge of the world, which is to say he has a role in relationship to all human beings, not just in relationship to Jesus or believers. But what is not suggested is that all peoples are invoking the one God as Father. It is the "you" of the Christian audience that is praying in this fashion to this person.

2 Peter

There is only one passing reference to God the Father in 2 Peter, in the description of the transfiguration in 2 Pet. 1:16-18, where God is said to be the Father who conveyed glory and honor to "our Lord Jesus Christ." This would only be surprising if in fact the author did not see the Son as divine, but at 2 Pet. 1:1 he probably calls Christ God.

Jude

The epistle of Jude has only one reference to God as Father, in the opening greeting, which refers to believers being beloved by God the Father and kept safe for or by Jesus Christ (v. 1). The coupling of Father and Son is of course familiar, especially in opening greetings or in liturgical contexts.[59] The stress on the love of God for believers and his sustaining power and grace is not a surprise either.

---

59. See pp. 32-35 above.

1, 2, 3 John

The term "Father" for God does not appear in 3 John, but it does indeed occur in 1 and 2 John in ways that comport with what we have already seen in the Fourth Gospel. In 1 Jn. 1:2 we hear about the eternal life that was with the Father, and in 1 Jn. 1:3 we hear about the koinonia of believers being with the Father and with his Son Jesus Christ. Note the characteristic Johannine emphasis on Jesus being his Son while we are God's children (see 2:1). At 2:1 Jesus is said to be our advocate with the Father when we sin. The mediatorial relationship between believers and the Father that Jesus plays is stressed here just as in the Fourth Gospel. As in that Gospel we hear at 1 Jn. 2:14 that it is God's children who know the Father and love him while 2:15 goes on to add "the love of the Father is not in those who love the world." There are some things in this world that do not come from the Father — namely lust, envy, false pride, and greed (2:16).

As is well known, the author of 1 John is very concerned about his charges making a good confession, and so he stresses at 2:22-23: "This is the antichrist, the one who denies the Father and the Son. No one who denies the Son has the Father, everyone who confesses the Son has the Father also." As in the Fourth Gospel, the denial of the Son leads to not having a relationship with the Father, and the reverse of this is also true. This again stresses the crucial mediatorial role of Jesus. 1 Jn. 4:14 further stresses that "the Father has sent his Son as the Savior of the world." The Son as agent or emissary is found here as in the Fourth Gospel. The Father is the sender, the Son his trusted agent.

Unlike 1 John, 2 John is a genuine letter, and as in various other NT letters we find a reference to God the Father. He is the one who sends the believers grace, mercy, and peace; and notice that immediately thereafter it is said to also come from Jesus Christ, the Father's Son (v. 3). Notice the stress on Jesus being the Son while again believers are simply children of God (v. 1). The unique relationship between Father and Son is again stressed as in the Gospel. 2 Jn. v. 9 indicates that whoever abides in the teaching of Christ has both the Father and the Son. The relationship with the Father comes through the Son, and is maintained by abiding in the Son's teachings.

Revelation

There are surprisingly few references to God as Father in the book of Revelation, four to be precise, and they are all in the first four chapters of the book.[60] Rev. 1:6 is the first of these references and is in some ways the most interesting one. Jesus is said to be the one who set believers free, making them a kingdom and priests serving "his God and Father." Here we have confirmed what we speculated earlier about the phrase in the Petrine corpus. The Father is said to be Jesus' God, and the focus here is on God being the Father of Jesus, not on his being the Father of believers. This comports with the almost exclusive focus in the Johannine corpus on the Father-Son relationship rather than the Father-sons and daughters relationship, when Father language appears.

In the address of the Jesus of the vision to the churches in Asia Minor, Jesus refers in Rev. 2:27 to "my Father," from whom he received authority. This sounds the Johannine note, already familiar from the Fourth Gospel, of the functional subordination of the Son to the Father, and the fact that he is an empowered and authorized agent of the Father. At 3:5, Jesus is heard to say that if the Christians persevere through the persecution and suffering they are enduring, he personally "will confess your name before my Father and before his angels." Again the unique relationship of the Son to the Father is accentuated. He stands in a position of influence in heaven, and can speak on behalf of his followers before the Father and the heavenly court. The final reference to the Father again comes from Jesus' lips at 3:21 and promises believers a place in heaven sitting with Jesus on his throne, just as "I myself conquered and sat down with my Father on his throne." There are several dimensions to this comparison. First, believers are not said to sit with the Father on the Father's throne. Only the Son could do that. And yet they can sit with the Son on his (separate?) throne. The position of power and honor is granted to those who conquered, which in this case

---

60. Which is probably another small pointer in the direction of the conclusion that John of Patmos is not also the author of the Fourth Gospel.

means kept the faith and did the Father's will to the end of life, even when it ended in martyrdom.

Nowhere in Revelation is God ever called "our Father," and in the one reference to God as Father not found on Jesus' lips the Father is said to be "his Father," accentuating the unique and uniquely intimate relationship they had. It is necessary to stress the point that the Father language is used only by Jesus or in a context when the Father's relationship to the Son is mentioned by John. This simply further supports the conclusion that Father language tends to appear where Son language shows up. The higher the Sonship Christology of the author, the more likely Father language will be brought into the discussion.

VI. Conclusions

A. Summary of Major Points

Contrary to the Old Testament, which was written from the Father's point of view, believers came to understand the Father through Jesus, the Son in the New Testament. This distinct and intimate relationship between Jesus and God changed the disciples' language, their knowledge of God, and their lives forever. The intimate relationship between the Father and Jesus provides the central focal point for uncovering and knowing who the Father was and is. For centuries God desired a familial relationship with his people, but it wasn't until Jesus that this door was thrust open. Jesus provided the picture of the prodigal's father, forgiving, loving, and compassionate, and always willing to accept his children.

It was this picture that provided the way for the children of Israel. It was this picture that established entrance into the family on the basis of faith and grace and not by works of the hands. And it was Jesus' intimate portrayal and relationship to the Father that enabled the disciples and all believers to call out *"abba,* Father" to their God. It is clear within the material provided that such language was not used by followers in the Old Testament. The *abba* language is introduced by Jesus and is prevalent among the writers of the New Testament. Paul's use especially ties fatherly endearment to God. Furthermore, Fatherhood for Paul was Christologically and eschatologically focused. Believers came to know God as Father through Jesus Christ and as adoptive sons were able to cry out *"abba,* Father."

The Synoptics concur that Jesus' relationship to God was unique. Jesus embodied the divine presence associated with the Father. This was unprecedented. God became the Father of our Lord and Savior Jesus Christ. Jesus not only provided a link for God to his children but became the only link through which the children could get to the Father. The relationship one had with Jesus became essential for the relationship one desired with the Father — a relationship underscored by the Fourth Gospel, which affirms that God is the source of life. The living Father sent the living Son.

The book of John sets its Christological orientation and tone from the very beginning. And as we have noted, the higher the Christology, the more prolific the use of Father language. Therefore it is no surprise that we find 120 uses of "Father" in the book of John. The author wants the reader to know from the outset that the Son comes directly from the Father, that he is the begotten Son, not an adopted Son. This is crucial to understanding that God's Fatherhood is carried out through the Son.

The other various epistles tell us more about the Father's nature. He is said to chasten, to be the one from whom every good gift comes, to be the impartial judge of the world and the conveyor of glory and honor upon "our Lord Jesus Christ." And it is in the Johannine letters that believers are deemed the children of God, adopted but united with the Father through the Son. Jesus is the empowered and authorized agent of God the Father, and it is through him that one must come to know the Father. Jesus gives us the clearest picture and the most intimate example. And it is through Jesus that the disciples and all believers come to know God as Father.

B. Implications and Explorations

There is frankly very little evidence in the NT to support the proposition that the proliferation of Father language for God in the NT comes either: (1) from the influence of the OT or early Jewish usage or (2) as a residue of the general patriarchal culture or of pagan practices, for instance, in the emperor cult. To the contrary, the evidence we have strongly suggests that the Christian usage of the Father language derives from Jesus' own usage of it and reflects the growing emphasis on matters Christological. The Father is seen through the eyes of the Son and in the vast majority of cases in conjunction with the Son. God the Father is most often referred to as Jesus' Father or the Son's Father, and only in a derivative sense, through discipleship to Jesus, as the believer's Father. On rare occasions the term "Father" is used to refer to God as creator of all creation and creatures.

One of the important motifs that generates this Father language is the notion of the Father as a begetter of the Son, and in an extended sense of humankind, particularly of believers who are "born of God." Begetting was and is indeed a male-specific function, and thus it is simply untrue to say that Father language as applied to God does not predicate of God any male-specific functions. While probably the majority of references in the NT to God as Father have to do with his love, mercy, compassion, and the like, which is to say they have to do with his being a good Parent to his already existing creatures and followers, there is a consistent stress in various NT witnesses on the Father = creator equation. The specific form that takes has to do with begetting, particularly in the case of the Son, as is made most clear in the Fourth Gospel.

It is then not just the fact that Jesus set a precedent for his followers of calling God *abba* or Father that provides an important warrant for Jesus' disciples to use such language, though that is true. There appears to be a theological rationale for Jesus' use of such language, namely that he believed God truly was the one who generated his human nature in conjunction with Mary, through a miraculous virginal conception. Clearly enough two of the Gospel writers also believed this to be true.

This belief could explain why Jesus speaks repeatedly, as no one else did, of "my Father" in heaven. Furthermore, it becomes apparent Jesus could not call God Mother, precisely because he had a human mother who had played her important part in his generation. In other words, this choice of language ultimately seems to come out of the unique relationship Jesus believed he had with the Father, a paternal relationship that by another miracle, the miracle of being born of God, believers could have an analogous form of.

None of this is meant to deny that at various points in the biblical tradition analogies are drawn between God's actions (and Jesus') and various feminine functions. Such remarks have to do with the divine activity, and they may also reflect the knowledge that God in the divine nature is spirit, and so neither male nor female. But an adequate explanation needs to be provided for why God is named and so characterized as Father but not as Mother in the NT.[61] The answer would seem to have to do with Christology and with Jesus being the font of Christian practice in regard to calling God Father, rather than to do with either patriarchy or the competing religious practices of non-Jews.

Helpful, but in the end unconvincing, is the attempt by Meye Thompson to plot a trajectory that suggests the NT use of Father language is basically grounded in OT and early Jewish usage, particularly in places where God is referred to as the Father of Israel.[62] Not only are such references too rare, mostly involving simply analogies, not the naming of God as Father in prayer or any other sort of direct address, but also what references we have almost never link the Father language to a particular relationship with one particular historical individual. Yet the NT usage almost always grounds the use of Father language in the relationship between Jesus and God. Even the Father-Son language for David or his descendant (2 Sam. 7; Ps. 2) provides but little precedent for such a singular focus in the NT. Furthermore, even these Davidic

---

61. Whether one wants to call "Father" a name or a nickname, clearly it is a label used to invoke or address a particular being. There may be some analogy with the way the term "Christ" became a virtual second name for Jesus.

62. See her conclusions in *The Promise of the Father*, pp. 156-62.

OT texts do not explain the "my Father, your Father" distinction we have remarked on in this chapter, or the fact of Jesus teaching his disciples to pray in a particular way to God as *abba*. The ecclesiological use of "Father" is grounded in the Christological one in various ways and repeatedly in various NT witnesses.

It has been complained by various persons that the use of the language of "Father" for God is insensitive to those who have come from abusive and dysfunctional relationships with their human father. D. Juel, for example, argues:

> Many within the Christian family . . . cannot speak the opening words "Our Father," without some intense experience of alienation. It is not only women who may have difficulty speaking the words; there are men who have no sense that there is a "Father" behind the dim unknown keeping watch above his own, and there are many who have no sense of the "we" presupposed by the Prayer. Language that earlier generations might have taken for granted may now require attention if the prayer is to serve as a vehicle for conversation with God.[63]

There are, however, serious theological problems with determining what God language we use on the basis of human dysfunctionality and relational problems. Of course there is always a need to be sensitive to persons who have been abused, but our naming of God should not be dictated by such human dilemmas. The appropriate response to such complaints is that there are good human fathers as well as bad ones, and analogies should be drawn with human relationships at their best, not at their worst. But it needs to be seen that for the most part the Father language in the NT is not an example of anthropomorphic projection on God of human fatherly attributes. To the contrary, no human being is a creator in the same sense as God, who created ex nihilo and created all sorts of creatures and things. To the extent that this Father language is

---

63. D. Juel, "The Lord's Prayer in the Gospels of Matthew and Luke," in *The Lord's Prayer: Perspectives for Reclaiming Christian Prayer* (Grand Rapids: Eerdmans, 1993), p. 56.

grounded in a theology of creation it is not a matter of projection on God of human attributes. Even more importantly, as we have seen, the Father language in the NT is grounded in a unique relationship between Jesus the Son and God the Father. This too does not involve a mere analogy between normal human relationships and those between Jesus and God. The terminology is grounded in beliefs about incarnation and virginal conception and the like, or in short, in a high Christology.

Even when Father language is used by Jesus' followers it is used because one has a relationship with Jesus and so with his Father. In other words, the ecclesiological usage is not primary but rather dependent on the Christological usage. It is not adequate to try and set the Christological usage within the ecclesiological usage. For example, Meye Thompson wishes to argue that "the so-called eschatological trajectory acknowledges the specific relationship of God the Father to Jesus, the son and the heir, who inherits from God the promises made to his people, who are 'heirs of God and joint heirs with Christ.'"[64] While there is some truth in this remark it says too little, for Jesus is also seen in the NT as not merely the inheritor of the promises but as the fulfiller of the promises, which is a divine task. In Jesus the promises of God are yes and amen. In short, it is not adequate to simply see Jesus as the first among equals in inheriting the promises. The Father language he uses is grounded in more profound Christological reflection and beliefs, that go beyond OT beliefs and practices.[65]

It is thus not adequate either to say "Jesus uses the language and imagery of scripture to promise God's faithfulness and love to his own peo-

---

64. Meye Thompson, *The Promise of the Father,* p. 158.

65. It is, however, true that Matthew and John are the more Jewish Gospels and have more of the Father language, which demonstrates that the proliferation of the Father language in such sources did not come through contact with the Gentile world and its religious practices. However, this observation does not prove that therefore the OT and early Jewish evidence can explain this proliferation. It may be true that in the OT God's Fatherhood is usually tied to the act of God's election of a people rather than creation (see Jer. 3 and 31), but this is not the case in the NT. The Son is not merely God's elect one, he is Son by other means — by begetting both in the eternal and human spheres.

ple and to call for renewed trust in God and love for one's neighbor. . . . Jesus does not create a new image of God or offer new propositions about God. He doesn't need to. Instead he calls for trust in God because God is faithful and wills to save his people."[66] But the language of Scripture does not include addressing God as *abba,* and Jesus was not merely renewing an already extant relationship between God and his people. To the contrary, Israel was to be seen as lost, needing to be called back from the dead to a new life and a new covenant. The radicality of Jesus' pronouncements was foreshadowed by the equally radical ones of his forerunner the Baptist, who flatly denied that talk of continuity or the divine-human relationship needing only a tune-up was adequate. Jesus wishes to call Israel forward into a new relationship with a God who can be addressed as *abba* if one will become a disciple of the one who has a unique relationship with that *abba.* "Father" is the only mode of address for God in the Gospels with good reason, and this fact cannot be explained on the basis of the rare instances where Father language is predicated of God in the OT and in early Judaism. The only adequate explanation for this phenomenon is the Christological one, both at the level of Jesus' own belief and practices, and at the level of the Christological beliefs and practices of the early church. The Father remained, in Christian thought throughout the NT era, in the first instance the Father of Jesus, and then through Jesus the Father of Jesus' disciples.

Meye Thompson, however, is quite right that the NT authors do not draw conclusions about human fatherhood on the basis of divine Fatherhood. Rather, the "ethical obligations derived from an understanding of God as Father are related directly to relationships with communities rather than within nuclear families."[67]

The reverse can also be said. Neither Jesus nor the NT writers say what they do about God the Father because of what they know to be best or true about human fathers. Their discussion is grounded in a particular set of historical relationships: (1) the relationship of Jesus with God; (2) the relationships of early Christians with God made possible by Jesus

---

66. Meye Thompson, *The Promise of the Father,* p. 160.
67. Meye Thompson, *The Promise of the Father,* p. 170.

and enabled by the Holy Spirit. The Father is seen through the eyes of the Son and on the basis of his teaching (both verbal and by his life example). It appears that the practice of disciples calling God Father only began after Easter and indeed after Pentecost. This is significant and suggests that the prayer and relational life with *abba* that Jesus had while on earth was only replicated in a derivative sense in the disciples once the Spirit was received. More could be said along these lines, but this must suffice for now. The interwoven nature of the relationship between Father and Son deserves further exploration by examining the Son language and other language found in the NT that predicates a more than normal human relationship between Jesus and God. To this we now turn.

QUESTIONS

1. The authors put forth the conclusion, which coincides with Seitz, that the new perspective of God as Father presented in the NT does not come from the OT perception of Father but from Jesus' own intimate relationship to his Father. This argument appears contradictory to that proposed by Meye Thompson, in which she argues that Jesus understood God first as Father of the people of Israel and as His father from that framework.

   A. Consider the merits and presuppositions of both arguments. Consult the text and write a brief outline of both arguments (that given by Meye Thompson and that given by Seitz / Witherington / Ice). Why are there so few references to God as Father in the Old Testament?

   B. In his argument, J. Jeremias emphasizes that it was Jesus' unique relationship that propelled him to use such a novel mode of address for God, i.e., *abba*. Does this argument lend support for or against Thompson's position? Seitz / Witherington / Ice? Why?

   C. How does Elizabeth Johnson's position cited on page 27 (note 18) influence your conclusions?

2. Explain what Jeremias means by "In Jesus' eyes, being a child of God is not a gift of creation but an eschatological gift of salvation."

3. The authors say that it is the Holy Spirit who enables one to make a true confession that Jesus is the risen Lord and this same Spirit who enables one to pray to God as *abba*. This same Spirit anointed Jesus at his baptism and was poured out upon the disciples at Pentecost. Furthermore, it is this same Spirit who opens the door to an intimate relationship with the Father, enabling the believer to pray as Jesus did, *abba*, to be conformed to Christ's image, and to become a child of God.

   A. In light of these statements discuss the meaning of "just because one is a creature of God's making does not mean one is a child of God in the true sense of the phrase." Refer to Romans 8:15-17 as part of your discussion. Use exegetical skills if possible.

   B. Reconcile your argument with the OT claim that the Israelites are the "children of God."

   C. When considering the book of Matthew, the authors state in contradiction to earthly fathers, "God's Fatherhood encompasses all he has made and begotten." Is this statement contradictory to the position presented in "A" above? Why or why not?

4. The book of John stresses the unity, love, and intimacy between the Father and the Son. Many families in society today experience similar father and son/daughter relationships. However, many families experience just the opposite at the hands of abusive, controlling, or neglectful fathers.

   A. To what degree should one's relationship with one's human father determine or influence one's relationship with one's heavenly Father?

   B. Can one overcome the experiences of the past to see God in a new light?

CHAPTER THREE

The Prodigious Son

———⟨ΦᏉᏉ⟩———

Since one of us has elsewhere discoursed at length on NT Christology, we do not intend to cover all the same ground in this chapter.[1]
Our primary focus here must be on the strictly theological side of the
Christological equation. This of course will entail a discussion of places
where Jesus is called God or Lord in the NT, but it will also involve examining some examples of the use of Son, or Son of God, or Son of Man
language where it appears that the divinity of Jesus is suggested. There is
in addition the use of terms such as "Savior" or "Alpha and Omega" and
a few other terms where a theological focus in the narrow sense of the
term seems clear. First, however, we must consider the Jewish context in
which such discussions as we find in 1 Cor. 8:6 became possible.

I. The Oneness of God in Early Judaism

It used to be the conventional wisdom of NT scholars that predication
of a divine nature to Jesus came about as a result of the impact of Hel-
lenistic culture outside Israel and the ideas that culture had about the
Divine. The assumption was that early Jews in tune with their mono-

---

1. See Ben Witherington III, *The Many Faces of the Christ* (New York: Crossroad,
1998).

theistic heritage would not use such language of anyone but Yahweh. The oneness of God ruled out speaking of multiple persons in the Godhead. This interpretation of what the Shema meant when it urged that "God is One" has recently been challenged by R. Bauckham, and we need to consider his argument here. It needs to be made clear that Bauckham is not merely arguing that Christ could be identified with special angels or personified attributes of God (e.g., God's Wisdom). He is arguing that the early Jewish definition of God could include the person of the Son without a violation of monotheism.[2]

First of all, Bauckham shows that the Jewish emphasis on the uniqueness of the biblical God found in the Torah, second Isaiah, later canonical apocalyptic texts, and in the intertestamental Jewish literature meant that even the greatest angels act as servants of this God. They do not share God's throne or rule (cf. Dan. 7:10; Tobit 12:15; 4Q530 2:18; 1 En. 14:22; 39:12; 40:1; 47:3; 60:2; 2 En. 21:1; 2 Bar. 21:6; 48:10). "So the participation of other beings in God's unique supremacy over all things is ruled out, in the case of creation, by excluding them from any role at all, and, in sovereignty over the cosmos, by placing them in strict subordination as servants, excluding any possibility of interpreting their role as that of co-rulers."[3] The notion of apotheosis, or the divinizing of a less than divine being, even if it was a supernatural being such as an angel, does not come into view in such Jewish literature.

Without a doubt, the factor that most made clear the creator/creature distinction in Jewish thinking was the issue of who was to be worshiped. The issue here is not whether there might be a few cases when some Jews may have venerated angels, varying from the dominant early Jewish monotheistic views, for there are.[4] The point is that such heteropraxy should rightly be seen as a violation of the tradition, which insisted that only Yahweh should be worshiped and no one else should

2. R. Bauckham, *God Crucified: Monotheism and Christology in the New Testament* (Grand Rapids: Eerdmans, 1998).

3. Bauckham, *God Crucified*, p. 13.

4. See the discussion in L. Stuckenbruck, *Angel Veneration and Christology* (Tübingen: Mohr, 1995).

be worshiped. One must not confuse occasional prayers offered to angels as worship, and it is worth noting that the NT itself clearly frowns on the worship or veneration of angels (see Rev. 22:8-9; cf. Rev. 1:17 and Col. 2:18).[5] "Jews understood their practice of monolatry to be justified, indeed required, because the unique identity of YHWH was so understood as to place him, not merely at the summit of a hierarchy of divinity, but in an absolutely unique category, beyond comparison with anything else."[6] The polytheistic way of dealing with such matters was to see the supreme God as the summit of the hierarchy of divinity, perhaps even the source of demigods and the like, but in the Jewish worldview the creator/creature distinction was sacrosanct. While God's spirit or word or wisdom could be seen as part of the divine being, distinct creatures such as angels or even highly regarded patriarchs were seen as not sharing in the divine nature or the unique identity of God.

It appears that the only real exception to this rule is found in some traditions involving the Son of Man. For example, in 1 En. 61:8; 62:2, 5; 69:27, 29 the Son of Man is said to exercise judgment on God's behalf, having been placed on God's throne; and at 1 En. 46:5; 48:5; 62:6, 9 he is worshiped. One could argue that this theology is actually generated directly from the implications of Dan. 7:13-14. This Son of Man is not said to be involved in the work of creation but rather in the future and final judgment of the world. What this last example shows is that while divine uniqueness is stressed it does not appear that this was taken to mean unitariness. Bauckham puts it this way: "The Second Temple Jewish understanding of the divine uniqueness . . . does not make distinctions within the divine identity inconceivable."[7] But this could not involve the violation of the creator/creature distinction. Apparently there would have to be internal development or distinctions made within the being of the one God, not the promotion of a lesser being to the status of divine for this to be consistent with exclusive

---

5. This last text may simply refer to worshiping *with* angels, i.e., ecstatic or visionary participation in the worship that is happening in heaven.

6. Bauckham, *God Crucified*, p. 15.

7. Bauckham, *God Crucified*, p. 22.

Jewish monotheism. It is of course perfectly possible to translate Deut. 6:4 as "hear, O Israel, the Lord is our God, the Lord alone," or the last clause could be translated as "The Lord our God is one Lord." In either case, the issue here is to make a statement against polytheism, not to make a statement in favor of the unitariness or undifferentiated nature of the divine identity.

Bauckham wishes to argue that later distinctions made by Christian theologians between matters of ontology and matters of function are not very helpful when it comes to analyzing early Jewish and Jewish-Christian texts. Indeed, reading such a distinction into these texts is anachronistic. This is so because "the unique sovereignty of God was not a mere 'function' which God could delegate to someone else. It was one of the key identifying characteristics of the unique divine identity, which distinguished the one God from all other reality. The unique divine sovereignty is a matter of *who God is.*"[8] Bauckham makes a helpful distinction between divine identity and divine nature. Identity involves both being and doing, especially in the case of God. Thus to predicate certain divine activities of Jesus is not merely to make some sort of claim that Jesus functions as divine. It implies that he shares in the divine identity, because only God was thought by early Jews to be able to create, redeem, or judge the world in any ultimate sense of these terms. Unlike Greek reflections on matters of divinity, Jewish monotheism was not primarily concerned with *what* divinity is (divine nature) but rather with *who* Yahweh, the unique and only God, is — divine identity.[9] Affirmations of the divine identity of Jesus can involve predication of either divine nature, or divine activities, or divine names to Jesus.[10] We will consider first Jesus' own use of messianic language followed by the use of *theos* and *kurios* language of Jesus in the NT, and finally the use of "Son" and "Christ" by the NT authors.

---

8. Bauckham, *God Crucified,* p. 41.
9. Bauckham, *God Crucified,* p. 42.
10. Bauckham, *God Crucified,* p. 42.

II. Jesus Named as God in the NT

While in the vast majority of cases in the NT the term *theos* (God) refers to God the Father, there are a few examples where the term is used of Jesus, six to be exact — Rom. 9:5; Titus 2:13; Heb. 1:8; Jn. 1:1; 20:28; and 2 Pet. 1:1. What is obvious immediately is that the use of the term *theos* of Jesus, while not plentiful, was nonetheless widespread. We find it in the writings of at least four different authors writing during the last half of the first century A.D.

The earliest and the most debated of these examples is Rom. 9:5. This text comes at the beginning of Paul's discussion of the benefits enjoyed by Israel. There is debate as to whether the verse in question should be punctuated "Messiah, who is over all, God blessed forever" (NRSV, NIV, NKJV, Jerusalem Bible) or "Messiah, who is God over all, blessed forever" (NRSV margin), or "Messiah. May God supreme over all be blessed forever" (NEB). In the last translation v. 5b becomes a separate sentence from v. 5a. Both the grammar and the context favor one of the first two of these translations.

Rom. 9:5a has the phrase "the Christ, the One according to the flesh" *(ho Christos to kata sarka)*. This construction, especially when compared to the similar Rom. 1:3-4, suggests that we should expect Paul to go on and speak of what Christ was according to some other category than "the flesh." Furthermore, the Greek phrase *ho on* ("who is") is normally a way to introduce a relative clause (see the parallel in 2 Cor. 11:31). There is then a high degree of likelihood that Paul calls Christ *theos* or God here in this doxological statement.[11] There is something quite natural about his speaking of God's Anointed One being blessed forever. One further grammatical point is of importance. *Theos* is used here of Christ, as in Jn. 1, without the definite article, whereas in the other NT texts mentioned at the outset of this section, the definite article is present. Without the article the term makes clear that Christ belongs to the class or category of being called God. It is a generic refer-

---

11. For further evidence see Witherington, *The Many Faces*, p. 109.

ence. With the definite article *theos* functions more as a title — he is "the God" just as he is "the Christ."

The other text in the Pauline corpus of relevance is Titus 2:13. While it might be possible grammatically to interpret the phrase to refer to two persons ("the glory of the great God and our Savior Jesus Christ"), when one compares Titus 1:4 and 3:4-6 this seems an unlikely reading, not only because elsewhere Christ is the only one called Savior in this letter, but more importantly because in 3:4 it is probably Christ who is called "the God our Savior." What is being predicated here of Christ is the divine redemptive work and in 2:13 the divine presence and power and holiness of God (= God's glory). Christ then is said to have divine characteristics and activities in this text, and therefore is described as having divine identity.

Heb. 1:8 is part of a catena of OT quotations, and in this case Ps. 45:6-7 is quoted and is predicated of the Son. He is said to be God and to be appropriately addressed as the one sitting on God's throne. This contrasts with what was said in early Jewish literature about archangels or special patriarchs. It must be borne in mind that Heb. 1:4 had just remarked that Jesus was exalted to God's right hand and so became far superior in name and position to such angels. As Bauckham rightly stresses, we should compare Phil. 2:9 at this juncture.[12] The name given to the Son is the divine name. It is thus not surprising that at Heb. 1:8 he can be said to be God, sharing the throne of God.

About Jn. 1:1 and 20:28 there is very little debate among scholars. The Logos or Word is called God in a titular sense in Jn. 1:1, and called both God and Lord in Jn. 20:28, two divine names. What is especially striking about the last example is that Jesus is addressed this way as part of an act of obeisance while Jesus is still upon the earth, albeit in a resurrected state. In the former text we have discussion about the preexistence of the Word before creation happened, and his involvement in the work of creation. All things were made through him and nothing was made without him. This again is one of the essential attributes of divine identity that occurs again and again in early Jewish literature —

12. Bauckham, *God Crucified*, p. 34.

only God is the creator. All things are made by God. Here the Logos is said to be part of the divine identity.

2 Pet. 1:1 has a phrase closely similar to what we found in Titus, which probably should be translated "of our God and Savior Jesus Christ," though it could be translated "of our God and the Savior Jesus Christ." This combination should not surprise us any more than the predication of the other divine name from the LXX, *kurios,* in 2 Pet. 1:2. The NT is full of examples where divine attributes, actions, names, and titles are all predicated of Jesus. Here again the emphasis is on the fact that Jesus assumes the divine redemptive functions. Of the normal triad of functions Yahweh is said to perform in Jewish literature — creating, redeeming, judging — all three of these are also predicated of Jesus in the NT. The functional/ontological distinction is not appropriate precisely because it was believed that one had to *be* the divine creator, redeemer, judge in order to function as such. Doing presupposed and involved being, which is why Bauckham is right to speak of divine identity (involving both) and not just divine nature (a sub-category within divine identity).

We must move on to the other divine name or title directly predicated of Jesus in the NT — Lord.

III. Jesus as Lord in the NT

The predication of the divine term "Lord" of Jesus in the NT is not in dispute, especially when one notes the numerous examples of this in places like the Pauline epistles. What is in dispute is the significance of this predication. We must consider several examples at this juncture. Perhaps the earliest example of importance for our discussion is found in 1 Cor. 8:4-6. Here we see a Christological reformulation of the Shema. We have noted the reformulated way that Father language and God language was used because of the introduction of Christ into the discussion. The same can be said in regard to the use of the term "Lord." Whereas in the Shema (Deut. 6:4)[13] the term "God" and the term

13. See above, pp. 67-71.

"Lord" were both used to refer to Yahweh, here there is a bifurcation such that "Lord" is used of Christ, and "God" is used of the Father. Paul in this context acknowledges that there are many so-called gods and lords (referring to perhaps both human and supernatural powers), but that for Christians there is only one God, the Father, and only one Lord, Jesus Christ. What could not be gathered from 1 Cor. 8 but is clear enough from other Pauline texts is that the phrase "Jesus is Lord" should be expanded to "Jesus is the risen Lord." The role of Lord is something Jesus assumed as a result of and after the resurrection. This conclusion is made clearer when one examines the Christ hymn in Phil. 2:6-11.

In this hymn we are told not only that Christ was in very nature God but also that he chose not to take advantage of his divine prerogatives. He took on a human nature and took on the role of God's obedient servant, even to the point of death on a cross. The second half of the hymn explains what God did on Jesus' behalf as a result of what Jesus did. God highly exalted him and gave him the divine name — Lord. Notice that it is only after Jesus' death and exaltation that the confession "Jesus Christ is Lord" is deemed appropriate. As Bauckham demonstrates, it is precisely the exaltation of Jesus to the divine throne that prompts worship, indeed in Phil. 2 universal worship of Jesus. The hymn in Phil. 2 is indebted to Is. 45:22-23. It is this very Deutero-Isaianic material which of course most stresses in the whole of the OT that Yahweh and Yahweh alone is God. Yet this is precisely the material being echoed in Phil. 2. "The Philippians passage is therefore no unconsidered echo of an Old Testament text, but a claim that it is in the exaltation of Jesus, his identification as YHWH in YHWH's universal sovereignty, that the unique deity of the God of Israel comes to be acknowledged as such by all creation. Precisely Deutero-Isaianic *monotheism* is fulfilled in the revelation of Jesus' participation in the divine identity. Eschatological monotheism proves to be christological monotheism."[14]

It would be possible to examine other Christological hymns like the one in Phil. 2 (e.g., in Col. 1:15-20 or in Jn. 1), but one of the authors has

14. Bauckham, *God Crucified,* p. 53.

trod this ground carefully elsewhere.[15] It would only add further confirmation that early on Christians predicated divine names and attributes and actions to Christ. Equally importantly we have evidence of Christ being the object of worship as God or Lord, and as being prayed to, even by Jewish Christians. Perhaps the earliest piece of evidence of this sort is the use of *marana tha* in 1 Cor. 16:22. In view of both Rev. 22:20 and v. 14 of Jude it seems rather certain that the proper translation of this phrase is "Come, Lord," a prayer born out of eager eschatological expectancy for the return of Christ. If one is a Jew, it is hardly likely that one would pray to a person seen as a mere deceased teacher to come! The evidence suggests that Jesus was seen as the risen Lord by even the earliest Aramaic-speaking Christians, and texts like Jn. 20:28 as well as 1 Cor. 16:22 suggest that Jesus began to be worshiped and prayed to very soon after he rose from the dead. I would suggest that it is in this context of the worship of Jesus as Lord, savior, indeed as God, recognizing there was already a divine Christology in place very early on and even among Jerusalem's Jewish Christians, that we need to re-evaluate the evidence in the Gospels where Jesus is called Son or Son of Man, or on occasion Christ and Lord. Somehow one must explain this remarkable Christological redefinition of monotheism by Jews, without simply attributing all the impetus to the resurrection of Jesus. There must be some Christological continuity between Jesus and his earliest followers.

IV. Son of Man, Son of God, and other Titles as Used by Jesus

Let us consider first the use of "Son of Man" by Jesus. We have already seen in this chapter that the Son of Man concept could be used to speak of an extraordinary being, one who can appropriately sit on God's throne and yet is not simply a manifestation of the Father.[16] One needs

15. See Ben Witherington III, *Jesus the Sage: The Pilgrimage of Wisdom* (Minneapolis: Fortress, 1994), pp. 249-94.

16. See pp. 69-70 above.

to consider not merely 1 En. 37–71 but also 4 Ezra 13, and one needs to keep steadily in view the fact that Daniel was clearly one of the most popular books among Jews in Jesus' era.[17] It is very intriguing that Josephus tells us that it was widely believed in the Roman Empire on the basis of a Jewish prophecy that a major king or ruler would come out of the east, a notion Josephus himself was to apply to Vespasian and so save his skin during the Jewish War.[18] It is even more interesting that while in his *Antiquities* Josephus works his way right through the popular book of Daniel, he entirely omits a discussion of the crucial material in Dan. 7:13-14 about the Son of Man. I would submit that this is because when he wrote this account in Rome and under Roman patronage after the disaster of the Jewish War of 66-72 A.D., he did not want to highlight earlier Jewish messianism which was grounded in this text.

Let us reflect on the crucial text in Daniel for a moment. First of all we note that a comparison is being made in Dan. 7:13-14. The author saw one "like a son of man." But who is this figure? Is he an angel, is he a human being, is he just a cipher for Israel? Dan. 7:27 provides one important clue, for it tells us that the Dominion will be given to human beings, not to angels; in particular it will be given to the people of God. Clearly enough from texts like Ps. 34:20 or 1 Macc. 1:46 the phrase "holy ones" can refer to human beings. But on the other hand in Daniel itself the angel Gabriel is described as having a human voice and appearance (Dan. 8:5-16; 10:16). In our view, however, this material comes from a considerably later time than the Aramaic portion of Daniel in Dan. 2–7.[19] One must ask, however: If the Son of Man figure is an angel who has not suffered with Israel, how does giving a Dominion to such a being comfort Israel? On balance the angelic explanation of the Son of Man figure seems not to account for all the evidence in the context. Nor does

---

17. This is clear not merely because of the numerous fragments of the book at Qumran, but even more telling is Josephus, *Antiquities* 10:267-68.

18. See now the discussion of this matter in Ben Witherington III, *NT History* (Grand Rapids: Baker, 2001).

19. See the discussion in Ben Witherington III, *Jesus the Seer: The Progress of Prophecy* (Peabody: Hendrickson, 1999), pp. 192-215.

the Son of Man = corporate Israel explanation convince in light of other material in Dan. 6–7. It will be remembered that the beastly empires are all said to have heads or kings, and it is these kings (heads), not just these foreign peoples, who are giving Israel trouble (cf. Dan. 7:27 and 8:21). There was of course a close connection in the ANE between the king and his people. The king was the representative of his Dominion and was seen as the embodiment and essence of his people. The material in Dan. 7:13-14 must be seen as contrasting a human and humane empire led by a human and humane figure with the beastly empires led by beastly leaders. As in 1 En. 37ff. and in 4 Ezra, the son of man figure must be seen as an individual ruler figure, not merely a symbolic cipher for a whole people. Confirmation for this interpretation comes from the fact that the Son of Man is given a Dominion; he is not that kingdom or its human constituents. The bestowal of a Dominion makes clear that the son of man is some sort of royal figure. Yet he is only said to be *like* a human being, and clearly when an everlasting Dominion is given to him personally (notice not to him and his descendants) some sort of transcendent figure seems to be in view. What sort of person is both like in some respects and unlike in other respects a human being? It is often maintained that Jews were not expecting a divine messianic or royal figure, but when one examines the trajectory of Dan. 7, 1 En. 37–71, and 4 Ezra, a more than merely mortal royal figure seems to be in view. We must keep this in mind as we consider a few Son of Man texts from the Gospels.

The phrase "Son of Man" is found eighty-one times in the Gospels, sixty-nine of which are in the Synoptics. All but three of these instances are found on the lips of Jesus himself, the exceptions being Mk. 2:10, Lk. 24:7, and Jn. 12:34. In addition the phrase is found only three times outside the Gospels (Acts 7:56; Rev. 1:13; 14:14), and within the Gospel traditions it is found in all the different sources (Mark, Q, M, L, and John). The case that on the one hand this was a phrase Jesus used repeatedly to characterize himself and on the other hand it was not a phrase that Jesus' followers used with any frequency at all after the life of Jesus or after the very earliest years of the Jerusalem church is a very strong one indeed.[20] The enigmatic quality of this phrase, which arises out of apocalyptic literature, doubtless made it impenetrable to Gentiles not familiar with the Hebrew Scriptures.

The first saying for consideration is a Q saying found in Mt. 8:20/ Lk. 9:58. On first examination this saying appears to be a comment on Jesus' itinerant lifestyle, but it may also have a more ominous tone, reflecting the way Jesus was rejected in various places and had difficulties finding any congenial place to make his base of operations. But there seems to be an echo here of 1 En. 42:1-3, which speaks about pre-existent Wisdom being unable to find a home on earth. This comports with the considerable body of evidence that demonstrates that Jesus did indeed present himself as God's Wisdom come in the flesh (see, e.g., Mt. 11:19).[21] The overtones of humanness and frailty are clear here, but something more ominous is implied in light of the echo of 1 Enoch — namely that Jesus was being rejected as God's Wisdom come on earth. He was living out the drama prefigured in early Jewish wisdom and apocalyptic material.

Another likely authentic Son of Man saying, in Lk. 9:44b, sounds the same note of rejection. This saying implies a violent end to Jesus' life. There is a play on words in the Aramaic original, which we can partially represent by translating the saying "The Son of Man will be delivered up into the hands of the sons of men . . ." (cf. Rom. 4:25; 8:31-32). This saying is in some ways reminiscent of the parable of the vineyard (Mk. 12:1-9), which we will say a bit more about shortly. The implication of the Lk. 9:44 saying is that the Son of Man is in the hands of God, who will be delivering him up. If indeed Jesus had some sense of messi-

---

20. It will be noted that the usage in Rev. 1:13 and 14:14, while coming from the end of the first century, comes from the pen of a Jewish Christian and seems to reflect a meditation on and allusion to Daniel 7 itself, rather than a development of the Gospel tradition. This material is nonethless crucial because in Rev. 1 it clearly depicts this Son of Man as a divine figure, having various of the attributes of the Ancient of Days who is also mentioned in Dan. 7. Furthermore, in Rev. 14:14 the Son of Man sits on a cloud with a sickle in his hand and a crown on his head and serves as the Grim Reaper, the judge of all the earth. Again the portrait is of a divine figure.

21. See Witherington, *Jesus the Sage*, pp. 117-208.

anic self-understanding it is not difficult to accept that Jesus would have believed that God had some purpose in his death as well as for his life. We must then consider the much controverted Mk. 10:45, which is found in our earliest Gospel.

It is now widely recognized by scholars that there was in early Judaism a belief that the death of a martyr could have an atoning benefit for other Jews (cf. especially various texts in the Maccabean literature — 4 Macc. 6:27-29; 2 Macc. 7:37-38; 1 Macc. 2:50; 6:44 as well as 1QS 5:6; 8:3-10; 9:4; J. T. Yoma 38b). Since we have this evidence and also the evidence from various different traditions that Jesus saw his destiny as Son of Man entailing a violent death (cf. Lk. 9:44b; Mk. 8:31; 9:31; 10:32-34; Mk. 12) it is well not to dismiss Mk. 10:45 as an utterance of Jesus. Like so many Jews before him, Jesus believed he was going to go into God's presence by means of suffering, and that his death would serve as a ransom for many. How does Dan. 7:13-14 fit into this scenario, if Jesus saw himself living out of the script of Daniel?

Scholars have long debated whether Dan. 7:13 should be taken to mean the Son of Man went up into heaven and received a Dominion, or whether he came down out of heaven on the clouds and received a Dominion from God on earth. The Aramaic text itself is ambiguous and could be read either way. But if all peoples and nations are going to serve this Son of Man, then it stands to reason that he is being given a Dominion on earth, which he will rule directly while on earth. This after all was the messianic hope of various early Jews — a royal figure would come on earth and rule in such a way that the Holy Land and the holy people would be re-established. Thus, the scenario Jesus seems to have had in mind was as follows: (1) he would complete his ministry as Son of Man on earth and would be rejected like Wisdom; (2) he would be delivered up and offer his life as an atoning sacrifice to God and for many; (3) God would vindicate him, raising him and taking him up into heaven; (4) at some point in the future he would return from heaven on the clouds to judge and rule the world, finally fully living out the promises made in Dan. 7. What needs to be borne in mind is that Jesus saw a wide variety of Jewish texts as coming to fruition in his life and ministry and in his future, including material from Is. 40–55 (Mk. 10:45 alludes to this in the phrase "a ransom in the place of the many"), material from Dan. 7, and wisdom material from 1 Enoch and elsewhere. Jesus interpreted his life and course of actions from these sorts of materials. We have independent confirmation for point (4) above in our next text — Mk. 14:62.

Mk. 14:61-62 needs to be read carefully. The high priest stands on the verge of judging Jesus, and asks him about his identity. "Are you the Christ, the Son of the Blessed?" Jesus' response seems to be in the affirmative,[22] but clearly he would rather talk of himself in terms of the Son of Man, for he goes on to say that Caiaphas would see the Son of Man seated at the right hand of the Power and the coming on the clouds of heaven. In other words, the one being judged would return as the judge. Both the position of the Son of Man in heaven and his role as the final judge are divine in character. That the Son of Man is presented as reflecting and participating in the divine identity comports with the earlier material in 1 En. 37–71 as we have previously discussed. Twice at crucial junctures in Mark when Jesus is offered messianic titles such as Christ or Son of God, which while royal would not likely connote a divine being, Jesus gives a qualified affirmation of such titles, but goes on to qualify his response by speaking of the future of the Son of Man (cf. Mk. 8:29-31; Mk. 14:61-62). In other words, Jesus seems not to be satisfied with a messianism that does not suggest what Daniel 7 suggests — that the final human ruler will also be more than human. If this is a correct reading of Jesus' use of the Son of Man material, we can certainly say that the beginnings of high Christology or divine Christology go back to the implications of Jesus drawing on the rich and complex trajectory of the Son of Man material. The rest of the material we discuss in this section must be read bearing this conclusion in mind.

If there was a dominant form of messianism in early Judaism it had to do with the coming Davidic monarch who would truly be the Anointed One of God. The phrase "the Anointed One" without further qualification would almost certainly mean the divinely appointed king

22. For detailed discussion of this point see Ben Witherington III, *The Gospel of Mark* (Grand Rapids: Eerdmans, 2000), pp. 383-85.

to early Jews (cf. Pss. Sol. 17:32; 18:37; 1Qsa 2:12-20; CD 12:23-24; 14:19; 19:10; 20:1). Here is the juncture in which we note that Jesus was apparently crucified as some sort of messianic figure; otherwise the titulus over the cross as elucidated in the Gospels is hard to understand. It read "This is the King of the Jews" in three languages, describing Jesus in ironic fashion as *basileus/melek/rex*. Notice that the titulus does not read *christos/masiah/christus*. The terms with more clearly political overtones are used. John Collins has recently and rightly concluded the following:

> Herein lies the anomaly of the messianic claims of Jesus of Nazareth. That he was crucified "King of the Jews" cannot be doubted. The claim to Davidic kingship also figures prominently in early Christian sources. The title *Christos*, messiah, is treated as a virtual name by Paul. It is unlikely that Jesus' followers would have given him such a politically inflammatory title after his death if it had no basis in life. . . . The messianic identity of Jesus must be grounded in some way before his crucifixion.[23]

This conclusion is correct, but the question is — In what way is it grounded? A close examination of either Mk. 8:28-31 or Mk. 14:61-62 suggests Jesus accepted traditional messianic acclamation but immediately qualified or amplified or recontextualized the discussion by referring to the Son of Man tradition. It follows from this that the Son of Man tradition must be the heart of the matter for Jesus, which in turn means that for Jesus lesser titles while accurate were inadequate. Nothing less than the human yet more than human figure would do for Jesus. This leads us to a somewhat more detailed discussion of Mk. 12:35-37.

This pericope reminds us once more of the biographical focus of Mark,[24] and thus of the great importance to him to answer in various

23. J. J. Collins, *The Scepter and the Star: The Messiahs of the Dead Sea Scrolls and Other Ancient Literature* (New York: Doubleday, 1995), p. 204.

24. On the authenticity and details of this pericope see Ben Witherington III, *The Christology of Jesus* (Minneapolis: Fortress, 1990), pp. 189-91. The material in the next few paragraphs appears in a somewhat different form in Witherington, *The Gospel of Mark*, pp. 332-35.

ways the question of who Jesus was. Notice that here, as in Mk. 8:27-30, Jesus takes the initiative when it comes to the issue of his own identity.[25] Jesus comes closer to revealing his identity in public here than in any of the earlier chapters of Mark, and it is not incidental that he does so in the Temple, which is to say in the place where people come to encounter their God and his truth and redemption. This episode in fact ends Jesus' public teaching, for from now on in Mk. 12:41ff. the teaching material is directed to the disciples.[26] Jesus points out that the scribes insist that the Messiah will be David's son. But, says Jesus, on the face of it this seems to contradict Ps. 110:1 messianically understood.[27] The precise phrase "son of David" is apparently not attested before Ps. of Sol. 17:23, but there is evidence from Qumran (4QFlor. 1:11-13) where the promise to David (see 2 Sam. 7) is interpreted in light of Amos 9:11 (cf. CD 7:16; B. T. San. 96b).[28] Here again Mark has followed the LXX with minor variations.[29] V. 36 is interesting, for it indicates Jesus' clear belief in the inspiration of the Hebrew Scriptures, as well as in the Davidic authorship of this psalm. J. Marcus also points out that the reference to the Spirit in this fashion suggests that the psalm is to be

---

25. See M. Hooker, *The Gospel according to Mark* (Peabody: Hendrickson, 1991), pp. 291-92.

26. See E. Schweizer, *The Good News according to Mark* (Atlanta: John Knox, 1971), p. 254.

27. It is possible, though not certain, that Jesus introduces for the first time the notion of understanding Ps. 110:1 messianically. See R. Gundry, *Mark: A Commentary on His Apology for the Cross* (Grand Rapids: Eerdmans, 1993), pp. 718-19. Against this conclusion is the fact that we may trace the beginnings of messianism back to 2 Sam. 7 and 22, which is to say it is traced back to David and his progeny. The author of Ps. 118 may have been looking forward to the ideal Davidic king, and called him *adonai* (not Yahweh), seeing him as being given the seat of executive power as God's right-hand man. It is not plausible to suggest that Ps. 110 dates from the Maccabean period, not least because it is found in early psalter collections such as the one at Qumran. We have independent evidence in Mk. 14:62 that Jesus used this psalm messianically.

28. See also D. Flusser, "Two Notes on the Midrash on 2 Sam. 7:1," *Israel Exploration Journal* 9 (1959): 99-109.

29. It is not true, however, that the wordplay in regard to the word "lord" depends on the Greek, for it would work equally well in the Aramaic — *amar marya le mari*.

understood eschatologically, prompted by the insight given by the eschatological Spirit.[30] The person in question is given the place of honor and power next to God, and the image of enemies being put under his feet is the image of the victor placing his foot on the neck of the conquered,[31] a not uncommon ANE gesture to indicate total domination on the one hand and total capitulation and submission on the other. It suggests an absolute power of life or death over the one in the prone position. This tradition of citing Ps. 110 messianically and eschatologically is also found in 11QMelch. We note here that it comports nicely with the material we have already noted in Dan. 7:13-14 where the Son of Man assumes such a role.

The riddle is offered up in v. 37.[32] How can David's Lord be David's son? Is Jesus here repudiating the Davidic origins of Messiah, as some have suggested? This seems unlikely since elsewhere he doesn't repudiate the title Son of David,[33] but he may well have repudiated certain popular early Jewish notions about the Davidic Messiah, for instance that he would simply be a normal, though God-empowered, human being like David himself. It is best to say that Jesus is repudiating the adequacy, not the accuracy, of assessing the Messiah by means of his Davidic descent. The point is that in Jesus' view the Messiah is more than, not other than, Son of David.

Notice that Jesus only raises, he does not answer, this question. The implication, however, seems to be that the scribes' notion of Messiah is far too mundane. He is a much greater figure than the original David, not merely a chip off the old block. Indeed, he is a transcendent figure,

---

30. J. Marcus, *The Way of the Lord: Christological Exegesis of the Old Testament in the Gospel of Mark* (Louisville: Westminster, 1992), pp. 132-33.

31. This text and its images were commonly predicated of Christ in early Christianity. See Acts 2:34-35; 1 Cor. 15:25; Heb. 1:13.

32. It is stressed in *Jesus the Sage* that Jesus' public form of discourse was most often sapiential in character. Riddles were of course one form of wisdom speech. Mark informs us that a crowd is present to hear this discussion (12:37), which in turn means this is not private teaching for the disciples. See J. Painter, *Mark's Gospel* (London: Routledge, 1997), pp. 167-68.

33. See pp. 75-77 above.

exercising lordship over even David.[34] The crowd is said to hear all this eagerly, loving to see Jesus poke holes in scribal balloons. We must indeed conjure with the likelihood that Jesus might be alluding to the fact that he himself was divine in dignity and origins and destiny.[35] The focus, however, is on the character rather than the identity of the Messiah in this pericope.[36] Here again, it is in how Jesus modifies or redirects the tradition that we see his own sense of messianic consciousness best. The human and yet more than human Son of Man was not merely David's son; though he was that, he was also David's Lord. Perhaps ultimately this sense of human and divine identity came to Jesus from his apocalyptic visions, or at least these visions confirmed his identity to him. We see him having such a vision at the beginning of his ministry as depicted in Mk. 1:9-11, and it speaks to him in terms of Sonship. We must consider this text in some detail now.

The narrative of Jesus' baptism uses language that suggests a visionary experience.[37] "The rending of the heavens is a common feature of apocalyptic thought, the underlying idea being that of a fixed separation of heaven from earth only to be broken in special circumstances"[38] (cf. Apoc. Bar. 22:1; Test. Levi 2:6; 5:1; 18:6; Test. Jud. 24:2; Rev. 4:1; 11:19; 19:11). In addition the voice from heaven speaks only to Jesus. This is a private experience and revelation (contrast Mt. 3:16-17). It is only Jesus who is said to see the Spirit coming down. Notice also that nothing is said about the reception of the Spirit by means of the water ritual. Rather, it is when he is coming up out of the water, or just after the baptismal act that the Spirit and the voice are encountered. The phrase suggesting analogy ("descending like a dove") is surely not

---

34. For an interesting and perhaps independent treatment of this same Ps. 110:1 in Christian messianic fashion see Epistle to Barnabas 12:10-11 and the discussion by Marcus, *The Way*, pp. 131-32.

35. See V. Taylor, *The Gospel according to St. Mark* (New York: St. Martin's Press, 1966), p. 493; I. H. Marshall, *The Gospel of Luke* (Exeter: Paternoster, 1978), pp. 746-49.

36. See rightly F. Neugebauer, "Die Davidssohnfrage (Mark 12:35-37 parr.) und der Menschensohn," *New Testament Studies* 21 (1974-75): 81-104.

37. See Witherington, *Jesus the Seer*, ch. 7.

38. Taylor, *Mark*, p. 160.

meant as a description of the form the Spirit took when coming down, but rather the manner of the descent, like a dove coming gently down for a landing.

Here there is a clear echo of Is. 64:1 where the prophet prays that the heavens be rent and God would come down so the mountains might quake at God's presence. Mark then is suggesting that what is happening to Jesus is an earth-shaking event. Jesus is anointed by the very presence and power of God, such that wherever Jesus goes and whatever he does the presence and power of God dwell in him and empower his words and deeds. He has in a sense what the sociologists call derived authority and power, but once invested it becomes an inherent authority and power that people recognize in Jesus (see Mk. 1:27). It may be debated whether we should see the voice from heaven as being like the later notion of the *bath qol,* the so-called "daughter of a voice." There is nothing derivative about this voice; it is God's own. The visionary and indeed apocalyptic character of this scene suggests the proper analogy is with voices that accompany visions, not the *bath qol.*[39]

V. 11 is again a composite Scripture citation involving Ps. 2:7 combined with Is. 42:1. The language is covenantal, denoting a special relationship between God and his Son. The word *agapatos* literally means "beloved," but it can connote "unique" or "only" on occasion. As God's special Son, God's special favor rests on him — including the full endowment of God's Spirit, equipping him for ministry. What we see here is the confirmation given to Jesus of who he is in relationship to the heavenly Father. In the Markan scheme of things it is no accident that it is only after this occasion that Jesus is tested and then begins his ministry. The baptismal event equips him for both of these subsequent matters. Jesus must know who he is, before he can do what God has assigned him to do, just as we will see later that the disciples must first know who Jesus is before they can understand about Jesus' mission to Israel. It is probable that Ps. 2:7 was originally used as a coronation ode on the occa-

---

39. See the discussion of this entire passage in Witherington, *The Christology of Jesus,* pp. 148-55.

sion of the elevation of a Jewish individual to the throne.[40] Whatever one makes of the OT quotation here, it is interesting that Origen sees in this scene a tableau involving the Trinity — the Father bore witness, the Son received witness, and the Spirit gave confirmation (*Against Celsus* 2:72). It was perhaps reflections of this sort about Jesus' baptism story that led some early Christian authors to the sort of Trinitarian stress and formulae associated with Christian baptism (Mt. 28:19).

Vv. 12-13 should not be separated from v. 11. No sooner had the Spirit come upon Jesus than it cast or drove him out into the wilderness.[41] Jesus must experience the full wilderness experience of God's people and in a sense the full consequences of their sin.[42] Thus he is endangered by wild beasts and tempted by a powerful adversary — the Adversary (Satan). In other words, Jesus' adversities were both physical and spiritual in nature. The wilderness is not merely the place of Israel's testing (Ps. 95:7-11), it was also the place of demons (Is. 34:14; cf. Deut. 32:17).[43] But it is also true that, like the experience of Elijah, the angels of God minister to Jesus while he is in the wilderness. Here Jesus first experiences the wilderness character of a fallen world. In various places in the OT the wilderness is associated with the place of the curse. It is not a place anyone would want to dwell, fit only for wild and ferocious animals. Note how the wild beasts are linked with Satan in Test. Iss. 7:7 and Test. Naph. 8:4. It seems unlikely then that we should see an Edenic motif in the reference to the beasts.[44] If the Lukan and

40. See P. Craigie, *Psalms 1–50* (Waco: Word, 1983), pp. 62-69; A. Weiser, *The Psalms* (Philadelphia: Fortress, 1962), pp. 108-16.

41. Schweizer, *Mark*, pp. 42-43.

42. S. Garrett, *The Temptations of Jesus in Mark's Gospel* (Grand Rapids: Eerdmans, 1998), p. 59, stresses "that it was [the spirit of] God who put Jesus into the wilderness to be tested. God has declared Jesus to be his son, and now God arranges for Satan to test Jesus to see whether he is worthy of that assessment. From this context, I infer that *the test was a real one,* in which Jesus was free to choose whether he would follow God's way or not, and in which his obedience could not simply be assumed. Otherwise the test would not have achieved its purpose of proving Jesus to be righteous."

43. For the motif of struggle with supernatural evil in the wilderness see J. Marcus, *Mark 1–8* (New York: Doubleday, 1999), pp. 169-70.

44. Yet the association of wilderness, animals, and temptation coupled with the

Matthean presentations of this same story are any guide, then it seems likely Mark has to some extent cast his narrative with Ps. 91:9-14 in mind, believing Jesus' experience fulfilled what the psalmist said: "For he will command his angels concerning you to guard you in all your ways. On their hands they will bear you up, so that you will not dash your foot against a stone. You will tread on the lion and the adder, the young lion and the serpent you will trample under foot. Those who love me I will deliver, I will protect those who know my name."[45]

The difference of course between Jesus and Israel is that he passes the tests he undergoes there and so is allowed to leave the wilderness and re-enter the Promised Land, indeed minister there. There is in this narrative the announcement of a major theme of this Gospel, namely Jesus' battle with the powers of darkness. It would appear that we must think of this episode as the account of Jesus binding the strong man (cf. Mk. 3:27), even though the Markan version is brief in comparison to the Q version.[46] Yet Mark's account is elliptical, for the nature of the test is not revealed. (Was it mainly physical and emotional suffering or mainly seduction that constituted the test?) It is then the fact of the testing rather than its nature that is Mark's concern.

There is another way one could read the Markan account of the temptation story. There is a story in Daniel about a king who wanders in the wilderness with wild beasts and there is mention there of angelic attendants as well (see Dan. 4:28-37). In addition, the issue in the story in Daniel is that Nebuchadnezzar had claimed to have built his kingdom by his own might and so is being given a lesson in humility and shown that in fact it is God who bestows kingdoms and titles. There is also the intriguing reference to Nebuchadnezzar being bathed with the dew of heaven, a sort of natural immersion (v. 33). But once Nebuchadnezzar

---

term "beginning" makes such a connection a possibility. If Genesis is the story Mark is echoing here, then Jesus is being portrayed as the latter-day Adam who passed the test. Is this a connection between the Markan and Pauline Christology? See Marcus, *Mark 1– 8*, p. 170.

45. See Garrett, *The Temptations*, p. 57.

46. See the helpful discussion by E. Best, *The Temptation and the Passion*, 2nd ed. (Cambridge: Cambridge University Press, 1990), pp. 28-60.

comes to his senses in the wilderness, having been informed about who really rules the world, he has his majesty and kingdom restored to him (4:36). It will be noted that after Jesus' experience in the wilderness he goes forth proclaiming the coming of God's Dominion. This entire episode, especially when coupled with the baptismal scene where Jesus is spoken to in the same terms David was, suggests that Jesus is being portrayed as a King, only one who is wiser than Nebuchadnezzar. But as we know, the ultimate sequel to the rule of Nebuchadnezzar is the rule of the Son of Man as described in Dan. 7. Perhaps here is one more clue that Jesus read his life out of the script of Daniel and related his experience in the wilderness to his disciples in such terms.

What is important to recognize in this story is that Jesus is called the beloved Son, which is another way to speak of God's only or unique Son. The language comes from Ps. 2, which speaks of the Davidic monarch in these terms. We have already seen in detail how Jesus' prayer life reflected a sense that he had an intimate relationship with *abba*/Father, a relationship in which he played the role of only Son.[47] Again we see Jesus reading his sense of identity out of the script of the Scriptures, but here it is in terms of Son rather than Son of Man. Perhaps we may say that in relationship to God, Jesus saw himself as Son, but in relationship to human beings, particularly Israel, he saw himself as Son of Man. There are no necessarily divine overtones to the use of Son messianic language in early Judaism. But if Jesus saw himself as God's only begotten in a more than adoptionistic sense, then such overtones would likely be present. We would suggest that Jn. 1, which speaks directly of the only begotten Son, and Lk. 1–2 and Mt. 1–2, which speak of it in another fashion by way of the story of the virginal conception, are simply making more explicit what was implicit in Jesus' own self-understanding, an understanding he shared with his disciples at various points. What we have seen in the discussion in this section is how the concept of Jesus having both a divine and human identity could well be grounded in the life of Jesus itself, particularly in the way he reconfigures various prophetic texts and concepts to explicate his own story and sense of mission

47. See pp. 20-25 above in chapter 2.

and identity. Bearing this in mind we must turn to a consideration of Christological language as used by the early church.

V. Jesus as Immanuel, Divine Son, Logos, I Am, Alpha and Omega in the NT

There is quite deliberately a back-and-forth character to the discussion in this chapter. We began by considering the concept of the oneness of God in Judaism, and the God language in the NT. We then turned back to see if that language might in some way be grounded in the words of Jesus. We now move forward again into the discussions of the church about Jesus, bearing in mind what has gone before. Our focus is on language that is theological in character, rather than simply messianic or Christological, if by the latter one means something less than language about Jesus as God or as having a divine identity. We will focus on a series of terms that have such resonances: (1) Jesus as Immanuel in Matthew; (2) Jesus as Logos, Son, Son of Man, I Am, and Wisdom in the Fourth Gospel; and (3) Jesus as Alpha and Omega in Revelation.

In chapter 2 we pointed out that Matthew and John have the most references to the Father, and also the highest Christological conceptions among the four Gospels. This is not a surprise when one realizes that the Father language is Christologically focused, or to put it another way: the more focus on the Son as divine and as the only means to the Father, the more focus on the Father as well.[48] Here we wish to focus on the Immanuel concept which is distinctive to Matthew's Christological formulation.[49]

The term "Immanuel" means quite literally "God with us." In Is. 9:6 it is said to be one of the throne names for the coming messianic king. The combination in Mt. 1:23 of virginal conception and predication of the name Immanuel quoting the Isaiah text in the LXX sets the reader on

---

48. See pp. 41-51 above.

49. On the indebtedness of Matthew to Wisdom concepts and for a comparison and contrast of these two Gospels see Witherington, *Jesus the Sage*, pp. 335-80.

notice that a very high Christology indeed will be predicated of Jesus in this Gospel. Lest we think that Matthew is simply saying that through Jesus God is present with his people, such a text in Matthew must be connected with Mt. 11:19 where Jesus is specifically called Wisdom come in the flesh, which is to say the very presence and mind of God come to earth. Thus when we hear in Mt. 12:42 that one even greater than Solomon is present in Jesus we are meant again to think of Jesus as Wisdom, for it is God's Wisdom, which Solomon sought and needed to be the great king. It is thus but a climax of this sort of thinking when we hear in Mt. 28:18-20 that the risen Jesus has been given by the Father all authority in heaven and on earth and that he will be with his disciples always, even to the End of the Age. In other words, Jesus does not cease to be present with his disciples simply because of the resurrection and its sequel. To the contrary he continues to be the presence of God among them, even as he was when he was born and lived among them. Again, the giving to the Son all authority and power and omnipresence is not a matter of the Father relinquishing a divine attribute or activity so that Jesus may take it up. Rather, the Son shares in the divine identity of God and therefore in God's almighty power and presence. Such a Christology must clearly be called theological in the proper sense of the term. Jesus is seen as God, for only God can be and do what Jesus is and does.

It has often been remarked that the Logos hymn in John 1 is the theological key to the Fourth Gospel. The remainder of the Gospel is to be read in the light of this Prologue, for this Prologue tells us of the origins and character of the Son. We learn that the one called the Logos pre-existed the creation of the universe and that creation involved him. We also learn that the Logos was God. It is interesting how this is put. It does not say "The Word was the God," for that might suggest that the Word exhausted the Godhead. Nor does it say "the Word was a god," as if there might be many such deities or demigods. In essence it says that the Word partook of the divine identity (God is used in the generic rather than titular sense here). One could convey the sense of it by translating it "God was indeed the Word."[50] Throughout

50. In the Greek we probably have a post-positive subject here, so that while the

the Fourth Gospel, knowing where the Son came from is crucial to understanding his identity. It is not just that he came down from heaven, but that his origins are in God — he is God's only begotten Son.[51] It is thus no surprise when we hear later in this Gospel that the Son can say and do the very same things that the Father says and does, and we also hear that the Son may label himself by the divine name "I Am," and that to reject the Son is to reject the Father. This tightly knit relationship is grounded in the fact that Father and Son are both part of the divine identity. What is important for our purposes to note is that this is not miles away from what the material from the historical Jesus suggests Jesus thought about himself. It is rather a drawing out in full view of the implications of some of the things he said about being Son of Man, Son of God, and David's Lord.

One of the major reasons for the difference of Christological portrait in John's Gospel in comparison to the Synoptics is that our author reads the tradition in light of the rich corpus of Jewish Wisdom literature. For example, the use of the term *monogenes* of the Son in Jn. 1 draws on Wis. of Sol. 7:22 where Wisdom is said to be *monogenes,* which we may translate as "alone in kind." In other words he is a unique being, which says more than, but includes the notion that he is the only (natural) Son of God. What is emphasized by such language is both the personal uniqueness of the Son and his pedigree. He is the sole natural descendant of the Father. The issue here is not means or manner of birth, but lineage. Jesus is said to be the only kin of God. One of the consequences of drawing on the Wisdom material is of course that the attributes of God which are personified as Wisdom are necessarily something internal to or inherent in God. Therefore when the author of John predicates such ideas of the Son this proves to be a natural way of making clear that the Son comes forth from the Father, and so is part of the very divine identity, just as Wisdom was earlier believed to be. It is definitely no accident that in the Fourth Gospel and 1 John only Jesus

---

above rendering follows the exact word order of the Greek, the Word is properly speaking the subject of the intransitive sentence.

51. On which see pp. 88-89 above.

is called the Son of God. He is not merely a chip off the old block, he is one of a kind, as the term *monogenes* makes evident.

Another good example of the influence of Wisdom material in John that increases the Christological and theological wattage of the Gospel is found in Jn. 3:14. As is well known, in this Gospel the Son is said to have come from and is returning to the Father. In Jn. 3:14 we have the first presentation of the notion that when Jesus is lifted up on the cross he has not only arrived at his "hour" (cf. 13:31 and 17:1) but he has begun his return or ascent back to the Father. In specific the Son of Man theology here is conditioned by what is said about the Son of Man in 1 En. 70:2 and 71:1 where Enoch ascends and then learns he is the Son of Man. These Enochian texts in turn build on 1 En. 42 where it is said that Wisdom descends to earth, then returns to heaven rejected. This same sapiential (and apocalyptic) influence from earlier Jewish literature can be found in Jn. 6:62 where we hear "What if you were to see the Son of Man ascending?"

If understanding Jesus in the Fourth Gospel entails knowing he is Wisdom come in the flesh, which involves knowing where he has come from and where he is going, then misunderstanding amounts to having mistaken notions about Jesus' origins and destiny. For example, in Jn. 1:45-46 even disciples and those who might become disciples believe they know who Jesus is by saying he comes from Nazareth and from the family of Joseph there. Or again in Jn. 7:25-27, the Jerusalemites know about the origins in Nazareth but they do not know where Jesus ultimately comes from (i.e., from heaven). Further examples of this sort crop up in Jn. 7:41, 8:41-48, and in 18:5ff. — the lack of knowing that Jesus is Son of Man/Logos/Wisdom who has come down from heaven.[52]

---

52. One must keep steadily in view that Jesus and the NT writers lived at a time after the cross-fertilization of Wisdom and apocalyptic in Jewish literature, which goes back ultimately to texts like Daniel and is carried forward in Wisdom of Solomon and 1 Enoch. Thus we need to understand that ideas bleed over from the Son of Man tradition into the Wisdom tradition and vice versa. Put another way, the blending of Son of Man and Wisdom traditions in the Christological reflections in John's Gospel are readily apparent and should not surprise us if we have read the larger corpus of Jewish sapiential and apocalyptic literature.

The same error can happen because of not knowing where Jesus is going. In Jn. 7:35 the Jewish officials misunderstand and think Jesus is going into the Diaspora to teach Greeks, or in Jn. 8:21-22 it is assumed Jesus is going to kill himself when he says he is going away. Even after Easter in 20:16-17, Mary Magdalene assumes the risen Jesus is back to stay. She wishes to cling to the earthly Jesus and simply resume the old relationship, whereas actually Jesus intends to ascend so that a new form of relationship can transpire between himself and his followers.

Throughout this Gospel Jesus assumes the roles normally attributed to Wisdom in her relationship to Israel (Wis. Sol. 10). For example, it is Jesus who comes into the world enlightening God's people. Moses and the prophets were inspired by this Word to write about his future earthly career (Jn. 1:45; 5:46). It is said of Abraham that he saw the Son's day (8:56), for the Son pre-existed. Isaiah even saw his pre-existent glory (cf. Is. 6 to Jn. 12:41). In other words, the Son existed before the incarnation and has had roles to play before that event as well. It is hard not to hear echoes of Wis. Sol. 10-11 here, for that text speaks of Wisdom aiding Abraham (10:5), entering Moses so he could perform signs and wonders (10:16) and offer prophecy (11:1; cf. 7:27), being present in the wilderness, and sustaining Israel with manna and water from the rock (16:26; 11:4; cf. Jn. 4–6). The Johannine Jesus understands himself to be the one who has aided God's people in their trials in all generations. Wis. Sol. 16:6 tells us that the lifting of the serpent in the wilderness is seen as a sign of salvation, helping us make sense of Jn. 3:14 which says that Moses lifted the serpent up in the wilderness, an event likened to the lifting up of the Son on the cross. Also, like John, the author of Wisdom of Solomon thinks of miracles as symbols or signs of salvation (cf. Wis. Sol. 10:16 and 16:6 to the sign narratives in Jn. 1–10).

There has been much debate about the "I am" sayings in John (cf. 8:24, 28, 58; 13:19) and whether they involve the transfer of the divine name to the Son. This question needs to be raised, not least because we are told explicitly in Jn. 17:6, 12, 26 that Jesus had indeed manifested the divine name, and that it is a name the Father gave the Son. "I Am" is said to be the divine name in the Hebrew text of Is. 51:12, which reads "I am 'I AM' who comforts you." We may also compare the Greek translation of Is. 52:6, which reads "My people shall know that I Am is the one who speaks." There could then very well be examples in John where the Son is given the divine name in these "I am" sayings. I would suggest this is likely the case in Jn. 8:58 and probably in 8:26 and 13:19 as well. Yet there are also various "I am" sayings that are not free-standing but involve a predicate — living bread, light of the world, the door, the life, the authentic vine (6:35, 51; 8:12; 10:7, 9, 11, 14; 14:6; 15:1, 5). The important point here is that all these things were already said to characterize Wisdom in texts like Prov. 3:18; 8:38; 9:5; Wis. Sol. 1–8; Sir. 24:17ff. The point of these sayings in John that draw on this earlier Wisdom material is to show that whatever one truly longs for or needs from God's Wisdom can be gained from Christ.

Though scholars have often debated why we have discourses in John and not in the Synoptics, it seems likely that the comparison with Wisdom literature explains this as well. Jesus offers the teaching of the very mind of God, since he is God's Wisdom come in the flesh. Therefore he speaks in a format such as we find Wisdom doing in Prov. 8–9 and elsewhere. The Farewell Discourse in Jn. 13–17 is especially laden with language that encourages the identification of Jesus with Wisdom. Sirach 4:11-13 is especially helpful at this juncture where it says (1) Wisdom teaches her children (Jn. 14–16); (2) Wisdom gives help to those who seek her (Jn. 14:16ff.); (3) whoever loves Wisdom loves life (Jn. 14:15); (4) those who seek Wisdom from early morning are filled with joy (Jn. 15:11); (5) whoever holds fast to Wisdom inherits glory (Jn. 17:22); (6) the Lord loves those who love Wisdom (Jn. 17:26). Jesus' disciples in these discourses are called little children just as disciples are said to be Wisdom's children in Prov. 8:32-33 and Sir. 4:11 and 6:18. The above must suffice as a demonstration of the way the use of Wisdom concepts ups the theological ante in the Gospel of John and helps the expression of Christological monotheism. We find equally interesting expressions of Christological monotheism in Revelation, to which we now turn.

One of the most interesting features of the book of Revelation that is of relevance to our discussion is the way the phrase "Alpha and Omega" is used. In Rev. 1:8 it is not clear whether the reference is to God or to Christ, though probably it is God. However, at Rev. 1:17-18

Christ is clearly referred to as "the First and the Last." At Rev. 21:6 it also appears to be God who is called "the Alpha and Omega," but at Rev. 22:13 Christ is called this. Christ at 1:17-18 is the one who was dead and is now alive forever and has in his hands the keys of Death and Hades and who holds the churches in the palm of his hand. What we see here, which is part of a pattern of predicating of Christ the same thing that is predicated of God in various parts of the NT, is very revealing. To call Christ "the Alpha and Omega" suggests that he precedes all things as does the Father and originates all things as creator, but also he is the fulfiller, bringing all things to their eschatological climax.[53] Rev. 3:14 comports with this: we hear there that Christ is the origin of God's creation. It needs also to be stressed that when Christ is called "the First and the Last" at Rev. 1:17-18 this seems to be an echo of Is. 44:6 and 48:12 where it is the divine self-designation of Yahweh, and it is used to bolster the claim that there is no God other than Yahweh. In other words, the very phrase used to stress the exclusive nature of Jewish monotheism is used here to indicate that Christ shares in the divine identity without violating exclusive monotheism. The reference to Christ as "the Last" (Omega) probably alludes to his role as final judge, which Revelation so vividly depicts. Bauckham's conclusion about this Alpha and Omega/First and Last material bears repeating. This language is "a way of stating unambiguously that Jesus belongs to the fullness of the eternal being of God, [which] . . . surpasses anything in the [rest of the] New Testament."[54]

It is precisely because Jesus is included in John of Patmos's definition of God, that he is seen as a very appropriate object of worship. In Rev. 5 we are introduced to the dominant image for Christ in this book — Christ the Lamb. At Rev. 5:8 the Lamb, who triumphed through his death and resurrection, is the focus of the heavenly circle of worship, which includes worship by the living creatures, the elders, and the representatives of all kinds of creatures, both animals and humans (cf. 5:6 to

---

53. See on this R. Bauckham, *The Theology of the Book of Revelation* (Cambridge: Cambridge University Press, 1993), p. 55.

54. Bauckham, *The Theology of the Book of Revelation*, p. 57.

7:17). It is as slain Lamb that this Lamb conquers and then judges with righteous anger (6:16). The worship of the Lamb is not distinct from the worship of God, but rather is seen as a part of it. The doxology in Rev. 1:5-6 must be compared to other similar doxologies about Christ in 2 Tim. 4:8 and 2 Pet. 3:18, which likely indicate that Christ was indeed an object of worship as deity in various early Christian communities.

The author of Revelation seems primarily indebted to a profound reading of the prophetic texts of the OT in his Christocentric theology, but there is also some evidence that he knew and drew on some of the Jewish Wisdom corpus, specifically Wis. Sol. 18:16ff. In Rev. 19:11ff. the conquering warrior is called the Word of God. There is surely an allusion to the Wis. Sol. text where the Word/Wisdom leaps from heaven with a sharp sword. In another Word-centered text in Rev. 5 we also discover that Christ is the one in whose hands the Book of Life rests, and he is the only one worthy enough to open the scrolls that disclose God's future plan and will. In such examples it seems clear that Christ not only functions as deity but it was believed that since only God could do some of the things Christ does in regard to creating, redeeming, and judging, Christ must be seen as part of the divine identity and thus worthy of worship.

The author has no trouble juxtaposing the human and divine attributes of Christ. In Rev. 3:7 Christ is said to be the one who holds the key of David, and in Rev. 5:5 he is seen as the Lion of the tribe of Judah and the Root of David. But in the very same context as the first reference, in Rev. 3:14 Christ is called the ruler not merely of Israel but of all God's creation. Christ is also not merely savior of the saved, but also judge of the wicked. At Rev. 11:15 we are told that the kingdom of this world has become the kingdom of God and his Christ, and Christ will reign in it forever. A text like this shows that our author is not guilty of Christomonism, though clearly Christ is included alongside of the Father within his definition of God. This text seems to reflect the same sort of thinking we have found in 1 Cor. 8:6.[55] At the end of Rev. 21 we are told that Christ and the Father will be the temple and glory of God's

---

55. See pp. 73-74 above.

people and that they will dwell together forever. Christ is seen in this book as at once Lion, Lamb, and Lord and various other things as well. What happens in this book seems characteristic of what has happened in the Fourth Gospel as well. While Jewish terms like "Son of God" in themselves would not necessarily convey the notion of a divine being, in their new Christian context these notions have been taken up into a larger whole, and the terminology has been somewhat transformed in light of the belief that Christ participates in the divine identity.

VI. Conclusions

In this chapter we have come to understand the Christological side of our equation by examining the various titles used throughout the New Testament for Jesus. We considered Jesus' own use of messianic language as well as the use of *theos, kurios,* "Son," and "Christ" by the writers of the New Testament. The examination of *theos* has shown that Jesus was credited with performing divine redemptive works and exemplified the presence, power, and holiness of God. Our analysis of *kurios* lends credence and support to Jesus' divine identity while helping to refute the idea that Jesus was merely a messenger from God or an exalted angel. Specifically, Philippians 2 brings forth the high Christology of the New Testament while bestowing upon him the title of Lord assumed after the resurrection. It is this title that prompts worship and adoration. These examples show the divine Christology that was in place early on in the Christian community that was established by Jesus prior to his resurrection, a Christology that was initiated by language used by Jesus himself.

Through the use of titles in reference to himself Jesus started many wheels in motion. Son of Man was clearly a title implying the messianic undertones of the text of Daniel. As stated previously, this was the title Jesus used most often to describe himself, and for that very reason holds great significance in our analysis. It is determined that the Son of Man is not an exalted angel or metaphor for corporate Israel but rather someone who is like humans in some respects yet unlike humans, possibly even divine, in other respects. It is then significant that Jesus would use this phrase to refer to himself above and more frequently than all others. In addition, Jesus presented himself as God's Wisdom come in the flesh. These characteristics alone imply that Jesus had a definite messianic understanding of himself, a messianic understanding that takes into account a death that would be painful and involve suffering, but a death through which God's purposes would be served. And it is this understanding that sets in motion the trajectory of high Christology played out by the New Testament writers.

The Messiah was to be a son of David and part of the Davidic monarchy. The Jews were looking for a divinely appointed king. In ironic fashion they bestowed this title upon Jesus as he hung on the cross, a divinely appointed king. But, this kingdom could only come about through the death and resurrection of the king. Jesus accepted this position and the traditional messianic acclamation that was given him by referring to the Son of Man tradition. However, to Jesus the Son of Man would be more than, not other than, the son of David. Jesus became the transcendent figure, exercising lordship over even David and having absolute power over life and death.

Jesus is not only seen as the Son of Man but also as Immanuel, Logos, I Am, Alpha and Omega. Each of these titles has its own importance, bringing insight into who Jesus was and is. Each brings support to the divine identity. As Immanuel, God is with us in the flesh, walking and breathing among us and to the End of the Age. As Logos, Christ shares in creation; his origins are found in God. It is through this close connection and relationship that the Son is able to take on the divine name "I am." Jesus is the sole natural descendant of the Father — the only one who is human in some respects yet divine, more than human, in other respects. He has seen God's people through all their trials throughout the generations, and as the Omega will be there in the end. He is the Alpha and the Omega, the First and the Last. He preceded all things as did the Father, and he will be there bringing all things to their eschatological climax. Collectively these titles leave little doubt of who Jesus was to the writers of the New Testament. Therefore, our examination of the titles used by and for Jesus throughout the New Testament can only lead us to agree with Bauckham that Jesus can be included in the strict definition of the Jewish monotheistic God without violation of the principles of monotheism.

QUESTIONS

1. In section IV, the authors discuss the use of titles for Jesus. As a young adult Jesus would have been familiar with the prophetic texts of Daniel, Isaiah, Psalms, etc. It is presented that Jesus used these texts to interpret his life and course of action. However, it is also argued that the Son of God pre-existed, as did God's plan for him. How can these seemingly contradictory ideas be reconciled to resolve the debate between the influence of the text upon Jesus and Jesus' fulfillment of the text?

2. Daniel 7:13-14 is presented as a central text in the discussion of titles used by Jesus. In fact, "Son of Man" was used most frequently by Jesus to describe or refer to himself.

   A. Why is the sheer frequency of use by Jesus significant?

   B. How does this text include the use of the phrase "Kingdom of God"?

   C. Why might the disciples be reluctant to use the title Son of Man when referring to Jesus?

3. Lineage has been an important part of the Jewish faith since God's covenant with Abraham. This can be witnessed in the books of the OT as well as the records in Matthew. Matthew deals with the human lineage of Christ, but little mention is given to the divine lineage as discussed by the author.

   A. What is the significance of Christ's divine lineage as you understand it? Why does it seem less significant in Matthew but is given prime time in Luke?

B. What is the significance of Christ's biological lineage to the Jewish people / faith? How do the titles Messiah and Son of God tie into this significance?

4. It would seem contradictory to Jewish monotheism to include Jesus and the Holy Spirit in the sovereign personhood of God. Second Temple Jewish monotheism was understood as strict and inflexible, with a well-defined idea as to how the uniqueness of one God should be understood. Therefore, Jesus and the Holy Spirit must somehow be directly identified with the one God of Israel and included in the unique identity of this one God to form the Trinity.

A. How can the three persons of the Trinity, God the Father, God the Son, and God the Holy Spirit be the same in essence or nature and yet separate in personhood?

B. What was the Son's role and that of the Holy Spirit prior to the existence of Jesus? And, after the resurrection? How and why did these events change their roles? What does it tell us about God?

C. How is God's identity in Jesus consistent with his identity in the OT Scriptures?

CHAPTER FOUR

The Powerful and Prophetic Spirit

——◦◦◦——

The evidence we have thus far examined in this study must certainly lead to the conclusion that both the Father and the Son were seen as God by Christians of the NT era, even by the Jewish Christians who wrote all these documents. They did not consider their Christological reflections a violation of monotheism. Rather it was a further explication of the shape of the divine identity. But such reflections could lead to practical binitarianism — an approach that suggests there are only two persons in the Godhead. Here we get ourselves into murky waters, not least because the whole meaning of the term "person" in modern English does not have the same semantic nuances as the term it comes from, the Latin *persona*, and before that the Greek term *hypostasis*. When we speak today of three persons it is normal to think of three "separate and distinct expressions of self-consciousness,"[1] but neither the Latin term nor the Greek one necessarily carries such a nuance. The question of personhood becomes a pressing one when it comes to dealing with the Holy Spirit, who has often been seen in church history and even today as a force or a power or a presence of God, but not as a person of the Godhead.

Here again, as in our discussion of the Father and Son, it is not ade-

1. G. D. Fee, *God's Empowering Presence* (Peabody, Mass.: Hendrickson, 1994), p. 827n.1.

quate to simply look at the OT or early Jewish evidence in regard to discourse about the Spirit. A reasonable case can be made that when the Spirit of God is mentioned in the OT and in early Jewish literature what is simply meant is God on the move in our world, or God's presence active among persons, not a distinct person within the Godhead. M. E. Lodahl has even tried to argue recently that the Holy Spirit is not seen as a person in the NT, but rather what we have is simply another expression of the same sort of notions about divine presence as are found in the OT and in non-Christian early Judaism.[2] With Lodahl it must be admitted that: (1) there are some texts in the Synoptic Gospels that could be read this way; (2) there is a dominant emphasis on the Spirit's functions or activities in the NT. Nevertheless, there is indeed evidence in various parts of the NT, particularly in the Fourth Gospel and in Paul, that the Spirit is seen not merely as a power but as a person distinguishable from both the Father and the Son. What must be borne in mind, as in the case of the examination of the Father and the Son language in the NT, is that the emphasis must be placed on discontinuity rather than on continuity with non-Christian early Jewish reflections on such matters. It is the new thing that makes the decisive difference in the NT discussion of the Spirit, and this new thing involves treating the Spirit as a person. It also involves treating the Spirit as the agent of Christ. Of course it is true that we do not find a doctrine of the Trinity fully articulated in the NT. But the raw data for such a formulation can be found in the NT, not least because the Spirit as well as the Father and the Son are all treated as persons, and all are treated as part of the divine identity in the NT. We are not in the same difficulties as was the case when dealing with the Son, because of course the Spirit was never a human being, and thus there are no texts to eliminate because of their focus on the humanity rather than the divinity of the Spirit.

2. See M. E. Lodahl, *Shekinah Spirit: Divine Presence in Jewish and Christian Religion* (New York: Paulist Press, 1992).

I. The Spirit in the OT and Early Jewish Literature

As is widely known, both the Hebrew and Greek words for "spirit" *(ruach, pneuma)* can also mean breath or wind. It is thus a matter of context to determine what the term means in a particular instance, and sometimes even then the meaning is not clear. For example, in Gen. 1:2 there is a reference to the *ruach* of God hovering or sweeping over the face of the waters (cf. Is. 32:15; Ps. 103:30; Job. 33:4; 2 Bar. 21:4). Should we translate this "the wind of God"? This is certainly possible, but the translation "spirit" is equally believable, suggesting the presence of God forming things. Such references to the *ruach* in relationship to inanimate matter are rare in the Hebrew Scriptures. Or again in Ezek. 37:5 the *ruach* here seems to be the life breath that will animate the dry bones. The text should probably be rendered "I will cause breath to enter you and you shall live."

Far more common are references to God's *ruach* coming on persons, either to enable them to prophesy or preach (Is. 61:1; cf. Lk. 4:18; 1 Sam. 10:10), or perhaps to empower or enlighten them to fulfill some office such as king (Is. 11:1-4), or even to give them supernatural strength (Judg. 14:6, 19; 15:14) or supernatural transportation (1 Kings 18:12; 2 Kings 2:16; Ezek. 2:2; 3:12-14). Ps. 51 is a royal psalm said to be David's response to being confronted by Nathan about his sin. In the midst of this psalm the psalmist pleads "Create in me a clean heart, O God, and put a new and steadfast spirit within me. Do not cast me away from your presence, and do not take your holy spirit from me" (51:10-11). Notice here the distinction between the human spirit and the spirit of God. In the first instance the term "spirit" may not even be an anthropological term but may simply mean "give me a steadfast attitude," but the latter use of *ruach* is something different altogether. Notice the parallel between the reference to God's presence and God's holy spirit. It is true to say that this is normally what a reference to the spirit means in the OT — the presence of God in someone's life, or perhaps in a holy place such as the Temple.

There is a close connection between God's Shekinah glory and God's spirit. Notice for instance when Ezekiel has a vision of the new

Temple in Jerusalem we hear "As the glory of the Lord entered the Temple by the gate facing east, the spirit lifted me up and brought me into the inner court . . ." (Ezek. 43:4-5). There really is no substantial evidence from the Hebrew Scriptures that the spirit of God was seen as an entity or person separate from Yahweh. In each case the reference seems to be to the presence of Yahweh in a person or place that normally results in the giving of life or the prophetic word or perhaps healing. It is important to note that there was the notion that God's spirit would come on a person or place sporadically or from time to time, and could be withdrawn, particularly if a person or group of people sinned and became unholy.

The most common understanding of the spirit of God in early Judaism seems to be that it is the spirit of prophecy, a phrase that becomes especially commonplace in the Aramaic Targums. The spirit provides revelation and guidance (cf. Sir. 48:24; 4 Ezra 14:22; Philo *Som.* II.252) or wisdom (Josephus *Ant.* 10:239; Jub. 40:5; Philo *Vit. Mos.* II.265; Sir. 39:6), or it inspires prophetic speech (Targ. Num. 11:26-27; Josephus *Ant.* 4:119; Jub. 25:14), or it inspires praise or other forms of worship (1 En. 71:11; Test. Job 48-50).

There is also in early Jewish literature some speculation about an especially spiritually endowed messianic figure, for instance an Elijah-like figure (Sir. 48:10) or a messiah priest (1QS 9:10-11; Test. Levi 18) or a prophet like unto Moses (1QS 9:10-11 drawing on Deut. 18:15-16) or a Servant figure who could be a warrior (cf. Is. 61:1-2 to 11QMelch.). In general one can say that there is more talk about the spirit and the spirit of God's association with specific anointed figures in the later prophetic corpus (e.g., second Isaiah) and in early Judaism than in the older portions of the Hebrew Scriptures. But normally in early Judaism, as in late prophetic literature within the canon (see Joel 2:28-29), the reference is to a future dispensation of God's presence that prompts prophecy and the like. What we do not find in this literature really is the treatment of the spirit as an entity or person separate from God. Indeed, as a text like Joel 2:28-29 makes clear, the spirit is said to be "my spirit" by God, that is, God's very presence, and as such it can be poured out or withdrawn. Nor is the spirit identified as God the person. In other words, God has a spirit (presence); he is not said to be a spirit.[3] We find something quite different when we turn to the NT and find various places where the Spirit is spoken of as a person who has a will and a work to do. The surprise in the NT is not that the Spirit is sometimes spoken of in impersonal terms in the NT, especially when quoting OT passages such as Joel 2 (cf. Acts 2), but that it is also frequently spoken of in personal terms as well. This change in diction requires an explanation, and once again the explanation does not readily arise from precedents in early Jewish literature. The emphasis once more must be placed largely on discontinuity with the Jewish background.

II. The Holy Spirit, the Historical Jesus, and the Synoptic Evangelists

It has often been remarked on how seldom the Holy Spirit is mentioned in some of the Synoptic Gospels, particularly Matthew and Mark, and indeed how seldom the phrase "Holy Spirit" ever appears on Jesus' lips in the Synoptics. For example, in our earliest Gospel, Mark, we have a reference to the Holy Spirit by Jesus in Mk. 3:29 in the discussion about blasphemy, a reference to the Spirit inspiring David in a dialogue in Mk. 12:36, and a reference in Mk. 13:11 to Jesus' disciples speaking under the prompting of the Holy Spirit in the future (after the death of Jesus), but that is all. In each case the Spirit is called the Holy Spirit, but there is no real discussion about the Spirit in this Gospel, nor is there any promise by Jesus to dispense the Spirit. That promise is made in regard to Jesus by John the Baptist in Mk. 1:8, but Mark nowhere portrays Jesus fulfilling or promising to fulfill such a promise.

Again Mark depicts Jesus having the Spirit come upon him at his baptism, and being driven into the wilderness by the Holy Spirit (cf. Mk. 1:10 and 1:12), but after the first chapter Mark shows little interest

---

3. The comment in Jn. 4:24 that God is spirit probably does not mean God = Spirit, but rather is a comment on the incorporeal nature of God, or at least there is the implication that God is not a material being who could be tied down to one locale.

in the subject of the Spirit. It is striking that when the Spirit is spoken of, once by John, and three times by Jesus, the reference is to the Holy Spirit, but when Mark refers to the Spirit in his narrative the adjective "holy" is omitted (Mk. 1:10-12). This particular fact suggests that Mark was not likely to be Christianizing his sources in regard to the Spirit,[4] nor was he likely to be adding references to the Spirit in general that were not in his sources.

We may take it as likely then that Jesus did on occasion refer to the Holy Spirit, though perhaps rarely. C. K. Barrett, in an influential study, has argued that the reason for the paucity of references to the Holy Spirit in the Synoptics, and in particular on the lips of Jesus in the Synoptics is several fold: (1) "Direct emphasis upon the Spirit had to be avoided . . . because Jesus was keeping his Messiahship secret; to have claimed a pre-eminent measure of the Spirit would have been to make an open confession of Messiahship, if, as seems to have been the case, there was a general belief that the Messiah would be a bearer of God's Spirit."[5] (2) While there is clear evidence that Jesus received the Spirit at the outset of his ministry, "there is nothing to establish a similar relationship between the disciples, the Kingdom and the Spirit [during Jesus' ministry], even though this might have been expected. This is apparently because the Kingdom, though present, was not present in fullness of its power; it too like Jesus the Messiah, was hidden, and under constraint. Therefore the Spirit was the possession of Jesus, as Messiah, alone, and in him it was veiled; and therefore, strictly speaking, there was no Church before the death of Jesus. The general gift of the Spirit belongs to the time of the vindication and manifestation of the Messiah and of the Messianic Kingdom."[6] There is very little reason to dispute these conclusions, at least in regard to what is said specifically

---

4. Here we are referring to the fact that while the OT does occasionally refer to the Holy Spirit (notice the Psalm reference on pp. 103-4 above) it most often just refers to the Spirit, while Christian sources in the vast majority of cases use the phrase "Holy Spirit."

5. C. K. Barrett, *The Holy Spirit and the Gospel Tradition* (London: SPCK, 1947), p. 158.

6. Barrett, *The Holy Spirit*, p. 159.

about the Holy Spirit. One could argue that the disciples must have had some spiritual empowerment when they went out on their trial missionary trip (see Mk. 6:12-13), but this empowerment may have come through contact with Jesus himself (see Mk. 3:15, though the reference to *exousia* there may focus on authority rather than power), not through reception of the Spirit. The inability of the disciples to deal with hard cases of demon possession is stressed in Mk. 9:14-29, and it will be noted that nothing is said either in Mk. 6:12-13 or in Mk. 9:14-29 to suggest that the works the disciples performed were performed by means of the indwelling Spirit's power. To the contrary, what we hear about is the necessity for them to pray that God may act! (9:29). In fact, we hear of someone casting out demons in Jesus' name (9:38-39) who is not even one of the Twelve; nor has that person been authorized by Jesus. We may conclude that Mark intends to suggest that the Twelve performed mighty deeds during the ministry of Jesus by prayer and by the use of Jesus' name.

Though the references to the Holy Spirit are few in Mark, it is important that we analyze them rather closely. What we will discover is that when Jesus speaks of the Holy Spirit, he refers to the Spirit as a person, and not merely as a power or a force or even just as another term for the presence of God. For example, in Mk. 3:29 Jesus speaks about blasphemy against the Holy Spirit. One cannot blaspheme against an inanimate force or power. By definition, blasphemy is something one does against God. It is an act of sacrilege. It is also important to notice how closely Jesus identifies himself with the Holy Spirit. To say "Jesus has an unclean spirit" and to suggest Jesus' exorcisms were performed by the power of Satan is to blaspheme against the Holy Spirit resident within Jesus.

One need not conclude from this text, however, that Jesus simply identified himself with the Spirit. Indeed, the immediately prior references to the Spirit in Mk. 1 make clear the distinction. The Spirit is not Jesus; it comes upon Jesus at baptism. The Spirit then engages in a personal act — driving Jesus out into the wilderness. Perhaps here is the place to note that when John the Baptist speaks about the Spirit in Mk. 1:8 he draws an analogy with water — baptism in/with water and baptism in/with the Spirit are paralleled. This is consistent with the more impersonal way the Spirit is referred to in the Hebrew Scriptures — as something that can be poured out, something one can be filled with, a medium one can be baptized in or with. It is Mark and Jesus in this earliest Gospel who speak of the Spirit in a personal way, not the Baptist who speaks rather like an OT prophet.[7]

The second reference in Mark's Gospel to the Spirit by Jesus (Mk. 12:36) refers to the fact that when David spoke Psalm 110 he did so through the prompting of or by means of the Holy Spirit. The Spirit is the one who inspires prophetic words. While it is perhaps possible, if taken in isolation, to see this as a reference to an illuminating presence of God guiding David's speech or writing, in light of the earlier reference to blasphemy of the Spirit we probably should not do so. It is of course true that in both the OT and the NT the Spirit is the inspirer of prophetic speech, but Jesus here is reflecting a more profound theory of inspiration than we seem to find in the OT. Jesus is referring to an inspiration not just of persons, such as David, but an inspiration that results in an inspired or God-breathed text, which he could now quote as having divine authority — a Holy Scripture, not merely sacred speech or oral tradition. Jesus elsewhere in this Gospel contrasts the Word of God with human traditions (Mk. 7:13), and this theology of the Word likely

---

7. This brings up an important theological point that is often the source of much confusion. The more impersonal language and metaphors one uses about the Spirit, the more the tendency to see the Spirit as a thing or a substance or a power rather than as a person. This in turn results, from a Christian point of view, in bad theology. Thus for instance, sometimes Christians talk about receiving more of the Spirit subsequent to conversion, as if one received only a little bit of the Spirit at conversion. But if the Spirit is a personal presence dwelling within the believer and not just a power or a spiritual substance, one can no more have a little bit of the Spirit than one can be a little bit pregnant! The Spirit can certainly deal with increasingly more aspects of one's personality through time, renovating the mind, the will, the emotions, etc.; but believers, once they have the Spirit and provided they do not commit apostasy and so quench or grieve the Spirit, cannot be said to get more of the Spirit over the course of time. The language of "filled," "pouring," and the like, grounded as it is in the impersonal references to God's Spirit in texts like Joel 2, has led to inadequate theological reflections on the part of Christians about their relationship to the Holy Spirit and their spiritual lives.

stands behind what is said about the Holy Spirit in Mk. 12:36. The Holy Spirit is the person who inspired and prompted David to say what he did, which is now preserved in writing as holy writ.

The third reference to the Spirit is in some ways the most telling in regard to Jesus' own perspective on the Spirit. According to Mk. 13:11 the Spirit is the one who will actually do the speaking through the disciples when they are dragged before authorities. Jesus is speaking of a time of tribulation subsequent to his current ministry when he will not be present in person to defend or advise his disciples. Then they will have to rely on the Holy Spirit to do the talking! It is perhaps possible to parallel what is said here about the Spirit with what the reader has learned earlier about unclean spirits when they possess people. Notice, for example, in a text like Mk. 5:7-8 that it is the unclean spirit that speaks through the Gerasene demoniac. The difference between Spirit possession and unclean spirit possession is not that the latter refers to an impersonal force or power, for clearly demons were seen as personal supernatural beings with wills and the like. The difference is that the Spirit leads, guides, prompts, directs, and in general respects the personal identity or integrity of the individual in which the Spirit dwells. The unclean spirit by contrast coerces, dominates, takes over the control center of the person, simply uses the person to its own ends, even uses the person as a mouthpiece to speak its own words.

We must move on now to consider the Spirit language in Q, and so in Matthew and Luke, focusing first on what the Spirit language in Q tells us about Jesus' view of the Spirit.

There are again only a few texts from the Q material that help us to grasp Jesus' view of the Holy Spirit. Let us begin with a text that may not help us very much. Most scholars think that Mt. 12:28a/Lk. 11:20a in some form goes back to the historical Jesus. The question is — In what form? The Matthean form of the saying says "If I by the Spirit of God cast out demons . . ." while the Lukan form says "If I by the finger of God cast out demons . . ." Luke has often and rightly been called the theologian of the Holy Spirit. More than the other two Synoptic writers combined, Luke refers to the work of the Spirit in his Gospel, and of course even more so in his second volume, Acts. If Luke had had in his source a reference to the Spirit of God, it is truly hard to be believe he would have changed it to the more arcane "finger of God" phrase. There is another reason why this is likely the original form of the saying. It alludes to Ex. 8:19 (cf. Ex. 31:18; Deut. 9:10; Ps. 8:3) in a way that is characteristic of the manner in which Jesus echoed the OT in his own public speech. He does not quote directly, but alludes to a familiar phrase about a mighty work of God during the Exodus events that led to the Israelites' deliverance. Thus, it seems likely that we do not have a direct reference here to the Holy Spirit, though clearly Jesus is claiming to exercise the power of God, or to perform these exorcisms by God's power.

The Q saying found in Mt. 12:32/Lk. 12:10 has in both forms of the saying a reference to the Holy Spirit, and it seems very likely indeed to have come from the Q version of the Beelzebul controversy where the issue of blasphemy against the Spirit is raised by Jesus. In other words, it appears likely Matthew has better preserved the original setting of this saying. This saying is interesting, not least because: (1) it clearly distinguishes the Son of Man and the Holy Spirit; (2) on the basis of that distinction forgiveness for blasphemy against the former is allowed, but forgiveness for blasphemy against the Spirit is definitely not allowed; (3) once more we see the Spirit treated as a person; indeed the parallels with the Son of Man are emphasized. Both are beings who can be spoken for or against. This saying is consistent with what we have seen already. The implication is that Jesus and the Spirit are working together, and a negative reaction to the ministry of Jesus and his mighty works is in fact a negative reaction to the work of the Spirit. Nothing here suggests that Jesus was speaking of anyone else having the Spirit other than himself, nor is there anything here about his dispensing or baptizing anyone with the Spirit during his ministry. Indeed, nothing in Mark or Q suggests Jesus ever spoke about baptizing anyone with the Spirit or sending the Spirit to the disciples prior to his death on the cross. Indeed, he seems to rarely have spoken of the Spirit at all. It is only in the Fourth Gospel that we hear about a pre-Easter promise of the Spirit, and then only really in the Farewell Discourses (Jn. 13–17), private discussions with the inner circle of disciples during the last week of his life. Even in that text[8] Jesus is not said to bestow the Spirit prior to Easter. Furthermore, it can even be disputed whether Jn. 20 speaks of such a bestowal before Pentecost.[9] We must consider the references to the Spirit in Matthew and Luke and ask how these Evangelists viewed the work of the Spirit.

The first reference to the Holy Spirit in Matthew, significantly enough, speaks about the virginal conception of Jesus within Mary. Mt. 1:18 stresses that the Holy Spirit was the means by which Mary came to be with child, though it is not clear who it was that "found Mary to be with child by means of the Holy Spirit." Joseph of course did discover she was with child, but the story implies that he did not know it was conceived by means of the Holy Spirit. The important part about this reference is that it indicates the creative power of the Spirit, an ability to generate something out of very little or nothing. In other words, the Spirit is seen here as God at work, as in the story in Genesis 1. According to Mt. 1:20 an angel confirms to Joseph that he should not refuse to take Mary as his wife, for her pregnancy happened through the agency of the Holy Spirit.

The next reference to the Holy Spirit comes in Mt. 3:11 where the one who comes after John is said to baptize in/with the Holy Spirit and fire. Scholars have debated what the reference to fire implies, but the First Evangelist at least seems to understand it to be a reference to judgment, in view of Mt. 3:12. It is possible then to read Mt. 3:11 to mean that he will baptize some with the Spirit, and some with fire, or to take both agencies to refer to the same action, in which case it refers to a baptism by fire through the Holy Spirit, which could be said to be purgative but also redemptive (burning up the chaff but gathering in the grain).

At Mt. 3:16 in the story about the baptism of Jesus the "Spirit of God"[10] is said to be seen by Jesus descending and landing upon[11] Jesus

---

8. On which see pp. 127-29 below.

9. On which see pp. 128-29 below.

10. Mark simply has "the Spirit."

11. The Markan parallel does not mention the alighting of the Spirit upon Jesus.

like a dove. Matthew then stresses in a way Mark did not that the Spirit not merely came down but in fact landed upon and stayed on Jesus. The Spirit's action is seen to be more gentle in Matthew than in Mark. For example, in Mk. 1:12 the Spirit is said to drive Jesus out into the wilderness, whereas in Mt. 4:1 he is said to be led by the Spirit into the wilderness. Leading is normally seen to be an activity of a personal agency, and so Matthew, like Jesus and Mark before him, stresses the personal nature of the Spirit.

There have been a few interpreters of Mt. 5:3 who thought Jesus was referring to those who were impoverished due to their lack of the Holy Spirit, but this is an unlikely interpretation for several reasons. The parallel in Luke, as is well known, mentions only poverty with no reference to "spirit," but more importantly this is not the normal way Matthew refers to the Holy Spirit. He either uses the phrase "Holy Spirit" or "Spirit of God." Furthermore, the Holy Spirit is nowhere else a subject for discussion in the Sermon on the Mount material this Evangelist derived from Q. As was the case in Mark, Mt. 10:1 refers to the authority/power Jesus bestows on the Twelve to cast out demons; he also refers to the curing of diseases with this power (contrast Mk. 3:15 and 6:7), but nothing is said of the Holy Spirit being the agency of these mighty works.

Matthew has moved the discussion found in Mk. 13 about being dragged before synagogues and councils back into a setting where it appears to refer to activities during the ministry of Jesus. Mt. 10:16-23 deals with a variety of possible scenarios, but crucial for our purpose is the reassurance that "the Spirit of your Father" will be speaking through them when they have to testify before Jewish or Gentile authorities (see vv. 18-19). Here is the first reference we have found to "the Spirit of your Father." This could be taken to mean simply the presence of God the Father within the disciples, but since Matthew's Markan source refers to the Holy Spirit (Mk. 13:11) and since elsewhere in Matthew, he does not use the Spirit language in an impersonal way as it is used in the OT, we should probably see a Jewish Christian usage here. The emphasis then would be on the Father as the one who sends or gives the Spirit to the disciples so they may utter testimony.

There is in Mt. 12:18-21 a quotation from Is. 42:1-4 that includes the line where God says of his Servant "I will put my Spirit upon him." This of course is referred to Jesus, but I would stress that since this a direct quote of the OT, it should not surprise us that the reference is to the spirit of God in an impersonal way. This is not Matthew's normal way of speaking about the Spirit, whom he does indeed see as a person, but since he was quoting Isaiah he was constrained by his source. The discussion about Beelzebul and blasphemy that follows in this chapter is interesting for the variety of ways the Spirit is referred to in a short span of verses. Mt. 12:28a offers the famous "If I by the Spirit of God cast out . . ." saying, but v. 31 refers simply to "the Spirit" who may not be blasphemed against (contrast Mk. 3:29 which refers to the Holy Spirit). In the very next verse, however, we have a reference to the Holy Spirit. There are then four different ways the Spirit is referred to in this chapter, but only in the quote from Isaiah is the reference to the presence or Spirit of Yahweh. In the other references an entity clearly personal and distinguishable from the Son of Man is referred to. The variety of usage likely reflects to some degree the First Evangelist's faithfulness to what he found in his sources (in this case Isaiah, Mark, and Q), but since he alters the Markan usage at 12:31 it cannot simply be explained in that way.

It is a remarkable fact but nonetheless true that after four references to the Spirit in Mt. 12, we have none in Mt. 13–21. The next reference to the Spirit occurs in passing at Mt. 22:43. Here the Greek literally says "How is it that David in Spirit calls him Lord saying . . . ?" This may be taken to mean "by the Spirit" referring to inspired speech, but it is striking that in Rev. 1:10 we find this same phrase, *en pneumati,* which we might call an OT or Jewish way of referring to God's spirit. The spirit is seen to be the atmosphere or sphere one enters (notice it is not the reverse that is being claimed, namely that the Spirit was in the speaker), which leads to inspired speech or a vision. The spirit then seems to be referred to in an impersonal fashion, but this is not entirely surprising since Jesus is talking about David's experience in OT times and is about to quote a passage from the OT (Ps. 110:1). There are no further references, personal or impersonal, to the Holy Spirit in Matthew until the very end of this Gospel at Mt. 28:19. In essence, this means that we have only one passing rather Old Testamental reference to the Spirit between Mt. 13 and Mt. 28:18.

Mt. 28:19, however, is something quite different from what we find in Mt. 22:43, or for that matter anywhere else in this Gospel. Here the Spirit is not only called the Holy Spirit and referred to in a personal way, but the Spirit is clearly said, along with the Father and the Son, to be part of the divine name. The noun "name" is in the singular. There is one God, who has a name of a tri-personal nature. Baptism is commanded to be performed using this tri-personal name. Here indeed we see the beginnings of explicitly Trinitarian expression about God. It is no accident that the First Evangelist portrays Jesus speaking in this way, *after* Easter and *as* the risen Lord who has been bequeathed all authority, power, and for that matter all divine knowledge by the Father. He is now able to reveal the full name of God, which is to say the full identity of God — Father, Son, and Holy Spirit (not merely the spirit or presence of the Father or the Son). We may be sure that early Christians would not baptize persons into a name that was viewed as less than divine, but Matthew here reveals the sort of Christian speech his own community must have used for baptism. He does not anachronistically predicate such speech of Jesus or others prior to the resurrection. Indeed, the disciples do not speak of the Holy Spirit at all during Jesus' ministry in either Mark's or Matthew's Gospels. We must turn now to Luke's Gospel, and see if indeed he deserves to be called the theologian of the Holy Spirit.

While we have seen that there is no promise of the Holy Spirit or dispensing of the Spirit by Jesus in Mark and Matthew, in Luke the picture changes considerably. For example, in Lk. 11:13 we hear Jesus say that the heavenly Father will give the Holy Spirit to those who ask, and the risen Jesus urges the disciples quite pointedly to stay in Jerusalem until they receive power from on high, which is called "what my Father promised" (Lk. 24:49). Interestingly enough, the place where there is most reference to the Holy Spirit in Luke's Gospel is in the birth narratives where clearly he is not drawing on Mark or Q. Thus a prima facie case can be mounted, quite apart from the book of Acts, that Luke does wish to stress the work of the Holy Spirit.

What is perhaps most interesting about this is that Luke, ever the historian, chooses to refer to the Spirit in the Old Testamental manner in his Gospel, speaking of a power or a presence or a force or something that fills a person, but there is very little in his Gospel that could be said to reflect the personal nature of the Spirit (but see below). By contrast in Acts, the Holy Spirit is seen to be an actor in the drama, so much so that he is one of the persons who hands down the Jerusalem Decree. Acts 15:28 reads "For it has seemed good to the Holy Spirit and to us to impose on you no further burden. . . ." Or again in Acts 16:6, the Holy Spirit forbids Paul to speak the Word in Asia on his second missionary journey. In this same text we see the further Christian stress on the connection between Christ and the Spirit. Thus at 16:7 the Holy Spirit is called the Spirit of Jesus. Luke knows that the more personal nature of the Spirit is a Christian concern and emphasis, and so he largely avoids anachronism in his treatment of what the characters in his Gospel narrative say about the Spirit.[12]

Let us consider the treatment of the Holy Spirit in Lk. 1–2.[13] The narrative in Luke begins with the story of John the Baptist's parents and the miraculous conception of John. In the midst of promising this child born out of due season, the angel says to Zechariah that John will be "filled with the Holy Spirit" (1:15). It is not clear whether we should see the reference to John's having "the spirit and power of Elijah" (1:17) as also a reference to the Holy Spirit or not. Since, however, John is seen as an Elijah figure in Luke's Gospel and since Elisha once asked for a double portion of Elijah's spirit (2 Kings 2:9), it seems likely that Lk. 1:17 does not refer to the Holy Spirit.

The next reference to the Holy Spirit in Luke's Gospel is perhaps the most famous one, found at Lk. 1:35. Mary is told by the angel that she will be miraculously impregnated, for "the Holy Spirit will come upon

12. This is very much like the way he handles the Christological matter of Jesus being called Lord. He may be called Lord in the narrative framework of the Gospel, but not in the speech material (see, e.g., Lk. 7:13). Luke is sensitive to the issue of historical anachronism.

13. See J. B. Green, *The Theology of the Gospel of Luke* (Cambridge: Cambridge University Press, 1995), pp. 41-47.

you and the power of the Most High will overshadow you." We may take this as two ways of referring to the same thing. The power of the Most High *is* the same as the Holy Spirit, which will both come upon Mary and protect her as God's power works within her. Equally Old Testamental is the reference in this birth narrative to the Spirit filling a person to speak or sing in an inspired fashion. We see this at Lk. 1:41 when Elizabeth is filled with the Spirit and proclaims to Mary that she is most blessed among all women. Perhaps a bit more personal is the description of Simeon, of whom it is said the Spirit rested on him (2:25), and that he is guided by the Spirit (2:27), and that the Holy Spirit had revealed to him he would not see death until he saw the Messiah (2:26).

In Lk. 3:16 Luke, like Matthew, has John speak of the one following him baptizing people with/in the Holy Spirit and fire. The one new note in the Lukan form of the story about the baptism of Jesus is the reference to the Spirit descending on Jesus in "bodily form" like a dove. This in turn leads to the uniquely Lukan statement at Lk. 4:1 that Jesus returned from the Jordan "full of the Holy Spirit," a Spirit that leads Jesus *in* the wilderness.[14] Thus Luke wishes to stress that Jesus was not abandoned by the presence of God while undergoing temptation and testing. Again at the end of the temptation scene we hear at 4:14 that Jesus returned to Galilee filled with the power of the Spirit, a note we find in neither Mark nor Matthew. All of this prepares us for the uniquely Lukan citation of Is. 61:1-2, which Jesus uses to declare that the Spirit of the Lord (i.e., Yahweh) is upon him, prompting and empowering both his preaching and his miracle working.

The next reference to the Holy Spirit comes at Lk. 10:21, which is uniquely Lukan as a comparison with the parallel in Mt. 11:25-27 will show. Jesus rejoiced in the Holy Spirit[15] that God had unveiled the hidden things to him.[16] Luke also has the blasphemy of the Holy Spirit

14. Notice the difference with Mt. 4:1 where it is said that the Spirit led Jesus into the wilderness, and Mark even says the Spirit drove Jesus into the wilderness.

15. Some valuable witnesses, including p[45], have simply "rejoiced in spirit," perhaps meaning Jesus' own human spirit, but the word "Holy" is well attested in some key witnesses and is probably original here.

16. The pattern of Luke adding references to the Holy Spirit compared to what he

contrast with the blasphemy of the Son of Man, which he combines with the promise that the Spirit will teach the disciples what to say when they are dragged before authorities (Lk. 12:10-12). The likely background to this saying is Is. 63:10, which refers to the rebellion of the wilderness generation grieving God's Holy Spirit.[17] It is interesting to compare Luke's reference to the teaching of the Holy Spirit with Mark, who says more bluntly that the Spirit will do the talking (Mk. 13:11), and with Matthew, who speaks of the Spirit of the Father speaking through them. In other words, Luke emphasizes the Spirit instructing the disciples, rather than just taking over the disciples and speaking through them. In all three cases the personal agency and nature of the Spirit are stressed.

References to the Spirit in the rest of this Gospel are quite scarce, until Lk. 24. Here we would simply stress Luke's indicating that Jesus claimed he would send the Spirit promised by the Father (24:49). Thus Luke ends his Gospel with an emphasis on the connection between the Spirit and Jesus. Throughout his Gospel the disciples are never said to be full of the Spirit; but Jesus, John, Elizabeth, and Simeon are so characterized, and promises are made to the disciples about receiving the Spirit in a way that distinguishes Luke's account from Matthew's and Mark's. More often than not thus far, Luke places more emphasis on the activity or power of the Spirit, rather than the Spirit as personal agent, though the latter is not entirely absent. None of the Synoptic

---

found in his source seems clear, but it is interesting that in his recounting of the Beelzebul controversy there is no reference to the Spirit, unlike in Matthew and Mark (see Lk. 11:14-23). It is also notable that at Lk. 20:42 David speaks on his own when the quote of Ps. 110:1 is mentioned, and there is no reference to the Spirit, unlike in the Synoptic parallels. It is also interesting to contrast Mk. 13:11 with its reference to the Spirit being the one providing the words with Lk. 21:14-15 where Jesus says about the messianic woes that his disciples must endure them and when they are confronted "I will give you a mouth and wisdom."

17. In general it must be said that second and third Isaiah seem to be the primary sources from the OT for Jesus and the Synoptic Evangelists when they are looking for ideas and phrases to describe the work of the Spirit. See M. M. B. Turner, "Holy Spirit," in *Dictionary of Jesus and the Gospels* (Downers Grove: InterVarsity, 1992), pp. 341-51. There are, however, plenty of echoes from extracanonical early Jewish literature as well.

Gospels have any significant amount of discussion about the Holy Spirit. It is not a topic discoursed on by Jesus or others. The audience is simply assumed to know what is meant when the phrase "Holy Spirit" or "Spirit of God" or the like is used. It will be well at this juncture if we continue to consider Luke's handling of this matter in Acts.

It has sometimes been said that the book of Acts should be called the Acts of the Holy Spirit rather than the Acts of the Apostles, and there can be little doubt that God in the person of the Spirit is seen as the primary agency of action in this book. Sometimes, as in Acts 2 and 10, the Spirit simply invades the human sphere and falls upon people before they even know what has happened to them, changing their lives in dramatic fashion. It is not by accident that the book of Acts begins with a retrospective that includes the reminder that even the risen Jesus operated on the basis of the Holy Spirit, for it says that Jesus was taken up "after giving instructions through the Holy Spirit to the apostles whom he had chosen" (1:2). The instruction to remain in Jerusalem and await the promise of the Father is mentioned twice (Lk. 24:49; Acts 1:4). An explicit connection is made by the risen Jesus between the prophecy of John and the baptism with the Holy Spirit (1:5). It is then in order to bear in mind that John spoke at Lk. 3:16 of baptism with the Spirit and with fire, and indeed this is how Luke describes the Pentecost event, which involves both tongues of fire and a filling with the Holy Spirit (2:3-4).

In some ways Acts 1:8 is the most important mention of the Holy Spirit in the introduction to Acts, for it involves yet another reiteration of Jesus' promise to his disciples: "you will receive power when the Holy Spirit has come upon you." What is most significant about this verse is that it does not simply equate the Spirit with the power of God in some impersonal way. To the contrary, the Spirit is seen as the personal agent who will supply the power the disciples so badly need. This power will enable them to be witnesses throughout the Mediterranean crescent.

In the speech made by Peter before the 120 believers the Spirit is once again spoken of in a personal manner. It was the Holy Spirit who foretold what would happen to Judas, speaking through David (1:16).

Throughout Acts the Spirit is indeed seen as the Spirit of prophecy, but also as the Spirit who empowers the disciples to work miracles as well.

The account of Pentecost has been analyzed and overanalyzed, but for our purposes only a few points are necessary. First, the sudden coming of the Spirit is described by analogies — it is aptly said to come like a violent wind (*pneuma* being the word for both wind and spirit). Again, the divided tongues are said to be like fire. These analogies describe the impression left on the disciples when the Spirit fell upon them. The description is given in rather impersonal terms not least because it is influenced by OT prophecies such as the one cited in Acts 2:17-21 (citing Joel 2:28-29), which speaks of a pouring out of the Spirit, as if it were a substance like water. We must bear this in mind because Luke has already made clear the personal nature of the Spirit in Acts 1:2 and 1:16. When he adopts and adapts language from the OT to describe the work of the Spirit, it tends to involve impersonal language. Acts 2:4 is an interesting example of the mixture of personal and impersonal language of the Spirit. On the one hand the Spirit is said to be the person who gave the disciples the ability to speak in other languages. On the other hand they are said to be filled with the Spirit, impersonal and metaphorical language drawn from the OT which refers to inspiration prior to prophetic speaking. Notice that it is said that the Spirit filled them all. This was not merely an endowment for a few leaders.

Luke certainly wishes to leave Theophilus with the impression that the falling of the Spirit on the believers had a dramatic and overwhelming effect. Thus the analogy with being drunk at 2:13, 15 is not a surprising one. The disciples are acting in an abnormal manner and are surprisingly loquacious, even in foreign languages. Peter explains the phenomenon by citing Joel 2. The disciples are simply Spirit-empowered and -enabled persons, just like Jesus through whom God performed deeds of power, wonders, and signs (2:22). Notice the way Luke puts the matter: God acted through Jesus, and in light of the portrayal of Jesus in Luke's Gospel this surely must refer to the fact that Jesus acted on the basis of the power of the Spirit within him, once the Spirit had come upon him at his baptism. In other words, Acts 2:22 should probably be seen as evidence that Luke was prepared to call the Spirit God, for it is by being filled with the Spirit that Jesus is enabled to do and say all that he does during the ministry (cf. Lk. 3:22; 4:1, 14, 15).

At Acts 2:33 we learn that it was when Jesus was exalted to the right hand of God that he then received the "promise of the Holy Spirit" from the Father and then in turn poured it out on the disciples, motivating them to speak. The connection between Christ and the Spirit and the Father is close here. They are all in heaven together, and the sending of the Spirit is handed over from the Father to the Son. There is an implicit Trinitarianism here; the assumption is that Father, Son, and Spirit are all part of the divine identity, are all together in heaven, and are all working together to enable God's people to spread the gospel. At Acts 2:38 we learn that in order for someone to receive "the gift of the Spirit"[18] they must repent, be baptized, and receive release from their sins. The promised Spirit is said to be for the immediately present Jews, for their offspring, and for all those who are far off (Diaspora Jews?), indeed for everyone whom God calls (2:39). Speaking in an Old Testamental vein, Peter goes on to urge his fellow Jews to repent so that "times of refreshing may come from the presence of the Lord" (3:20). The Spirit's coming is associated with the renewal and refreshment of life sent from the very presence of God, or put another way, conveyed by the coming of God's presence in the person of the Spirit. It is no less than God and God's presence that comes when the Spirit comes on a person.

Peter is depicted as a Spirit-filled person, who is inspired to speak boldly to the Jewish authorities at Acts 4:8. They had asked by what power or authority he was doing what he was doing, and Luke leaves us in no doubt it is by the power and authority of the Spirit. The Spirit inspires not merely boldness (see 4:13) but also educated and articulate discourse. The personal agency of the Spirit is again stressed at 4:25 where once more we find a somewhat familiar phrase (cf. 1:16): "Sovereign Lord [i.e., God the Father], who made heaven and earth, the sea and everything in them, it is you who said by the Holy Spirit through

18. Notice that though the Spirit is promised by the Father, it is not something owed to human beings. It is still a gift, even though its giving has been prophesied or promised.

our ancestor David. . . ." This is again interesting because it speaks of God working through or by the Spirit and through the human agency of David as well. The Father speaks by the Spirit and through the human agent. Again we begin to see an implicitly Trinitarian way of thinking about the way God operates.

Acts 5 contains the remarkable story about Ananias and Sapphira, who are accused by Peter of "lying to the Holy Spirit" (5:3). Here again the Spirit is seen as a person who can be spoken to. At 5:9 it is said to be "the Spirit of the Lord" that this couple had put to the test. Notice the close connection between the Spirit and God (or possibly "Lord" here means "Christ"). To put the Spirit of the Lord to the test is to put God to the test. The Spirit is clearly not seen as someone or something less than God. It is possible that the phrase here means the Spirit whom the Lord sent and now resides in Peter and others. Acts 5:32 adds a reference to the Spirit acting as a personal witness alongside the disciples in the testimony about Jesus; there it is also said that the Spirit is given by God to those who obey him. This suggests perhaps that "Lord" in 5:9 refers to God rather than Christ.

According to Acts 6:3, one of the essential criteria for selecting seven new leaders is that they must be "full of the Spirit and of wisdom." This may be an example of hendiadys, in which case the meaning would be full of the Spirit who conveys wisdom. At 6:5 we are told that the first person chosen, Stephen, is both full of faith and of the Holy Spirit. He is also said at 6:8 to be full of grace and power, and thereby enabled to perform great wonders and signs among the people. We here get a fuller glimpse of what the Spirit bequeaths. Not only does the Spirit inspire prophetic speech, it also conveys wisdom, faith, grace, and the power to perform miracles. Those who opposed Stephen's evangelizing nonetheless were not able to "withstand the wisdom and Spirit with which he spoke" (6:10). They were only able to commit libel by suggesting that Stephen was blaspheming. This is a significant juncture in the story: many Jews are about to turn against the gospel, and the alert reader who remembers from Luke's Gospel what was said about blasphemy against the Holy Spirit (see above) will realize the gravity of this situation for God's people. Again at the end of his speech at 7:55 Stephen is said to be filled with the Spirit, and on this occasion the Spirit inspires a vision, for Stephen sees the Son of Man standing in heaven. Thus the Spirit inspires not just words, but also visions.

Acts 8 recounts a new stage in the missionary work of the church, with the reaching out to the Samaritans. Philip, however, does not convey the Spirit to these people. Rather it is when Peter and John come down that there is prayer that the Samaritans might receive the Holy Spirit (8:15-16). Luke explains that as of yet they had only received water baptism, and had not yet received the Holy Spirit. The reference to prayer here is important, and should be compared to Acts 1:24–2:1. The reference to prayer makes evident that even the chief apostles could not dispense the Spirit at will from their own personal supply, as it were. Rather they must ask God to give it to others. Notice that Simon Magus asks these apostles not for the Spirit, but for the power to convey the Spirit (8:19), and is peremptorily turned down. The Spirit is said to be given through the laying on of hands, but this is only after prayer (8:15-18). This story is important because it shows that Luke does not necessarily associate the reception of the Spirit with the reception of water baptism. Indeed, the two are clearly distinguished in time and nature here, just as in the Gospel there was a distinction between the reception of John's baptism, and the reception of the Spirit through the action of Jesus. Yet of course on some occasions the reception of water and the Spirit can be nearly coincident in time as was the case with Jesus himself, and apparently also the Ethiopian eunuch (cf. Lk. 3:21-22; Acts 8:26-40). Notice, however, that we are told quite explicitly by Luke that the baptism of Jesus with water came first; then when Jesus was praying the heavens were opened and the Spirit came down (3:21b-22a). The sequence is close, but the water baptism does not convey the Spirit. The Spirit comes in response to prayer, as in Acts 8:15. Acts 8:39 ends this chapter by portraying Philip as a latter-day prophetic figure like Elijah, for whom the Spirit even provides transportation. The Spirit "snatched Philip away" and the next thing he knew he was at Azotus (cf. 1 Kings 18:46).

The next reference to the Holy Spirit occurs in the story of Saul's conversion. Ananias is sent on a mission by Jesus to Saul "so that you may regain your sight and be filled with the Holy Spirit" (9:17). Baptism is also mentioned at v. 18, but Luke says nothing about what the connection, if any, between being filled with the Spirit and being baptized in water might be. We may surmise that Luke believes that if one has the Spirit, water baptism should not be withheld (cf. Acts 10 below). The text is more naturally read to suggest a connection between a regaining of sight and the filling with the Spirit rather than a connection with baptism.

The summary statement in Acts 9:31 is interesting. The church in the Holy Land is said to be living in the fear of the Lord (i.e., God) and in the comfort of the Spirit. Notice the parallelism. The Spirit is not simply identified with God the Father, but is clearly implied to be personal in nature — capable of comforting believers. This theme of the personal nature of the Spirit is continued in Acts 10:19 where we are told that it is the Spirit that spoke to Peter after his vision, alerting him to the arrival of Cornelius's emissaries (also in Peter's recounting of the issue at 11:12). This can be seen in Peter's speech where he briefly rehearses the story of Jesus, and at v. 38 he tells how God anointed Jesus "with the Holy Spirit and with power." This may be an example of hendiadys, but in light of the personal approach to the Spirit in this chapter the two things should probably be distinguished. The Spirit is not simply impersonal divine power, but certainly can and does convey power to Jesus and others. V. 44 speaks of the Holy Spirit falling on all of Cornelius's family who heard the preaching. Peter recognizes this event has transpired because he hears them speaking in tongues and praising God. Baptism should not be withheld from those who have already received the Spirit. We have thus seen the order water then Spirit in Acts 8, and Spirit then water in Acts 10. We can only conclude that Luke is not trying to suggest that one particular order of things is normative. For Luke the sine qua non of Christian experience is receiving the Spirit, not being baptized, as seems clear from the case of Apollos in Acts 18. Perhaps the most important comment of Peter about the Cornelius episode is that found in 11:15, where he stresses that it was the same Spirit who fell on these Gentiles as fell on the Jews in Acts 2, and it happened to them just as it happened earlier in Acts 2 — unexpectedly and at the divine initiative. The contrast between water and Spirit baptism in 11:16 is also interesting. John offered the former but Peter says that Jesus promised the latter.[19] Notice too at 11:17 that it is said to be God who gives the gift of the Spirit to those who believed in Christ. We begin to see a close connection between preaching, believing in Jesus, and receiving the Spirit.

Barnabas is an important figure in Luke's narrative even before Acts 11:22-23 (cf. 4:36-37), but in Acts 11 he becomes even more important. The description of him as "full of the Holy Spirit and of faith" is the same as that of Stephen in 6:5, except the terms are reversed. The close connection between having the Spirit and having faith is stressed. Equally interesting in this text is the reference to Agabus, the Christian prophet who "predicted by the Spirit that there would be a severe famine" (v. 28). The Spirit is again seen as the Spirit of prophecy. Agabus reappears in Acts 21:11, this time in Caesarea rather than in Antioch, and performs the symbolic gesture of binding Paul. He remarks, "Thus says the Holy Spirit: 'This is the way the Jews in Jerusalem will bind the man . . .'" There can be little doubt from this last reference that the Spirit is seen as God, for the standard prophetic formula is modified from "Thus says the Lord" at this juncture.[20]

We find another example of the Holy Spirit speaking at Acts 13:2, where it commands that Paul and Barnabas be set apart for a missionary venture. Notice that it is said that this speaking transpires while the church is worshiping and fasting. Presumably we are meant to think that a prophet spoke these words prompted by the Spirit. It is also stated quite clearly that it is the Holy Spirit who sends these men out. Thus we see the Spirit acting like a person in two ways here — speaking

19. This is actually doubly interesting because of course at Lk. 3:16 we have a saying of John, but here Peter speaks of a saying of Jesus. Perhaps we are meant to think that what John said was later repeated by Jesus to the disciples. If so, Luke does not record such an event in his Gospel.

20. In fact the prophecy is rather inexact, as the Jews do not bind Paul and turn him over to the Gentiles. Rather a Roman in essence takes custody of Paul from the Jewish mob. It is the Romans who bind Paul and cart him off to Caesarea Maritima.

and sending others out. Yet we also hear of Paul being filled with the Spirit and given spiritual sight or insight into Elymas (13:9). This phrase about being filled with the Spirit, often compounded with something else, is very common in Luke-Acts, and we find another example in the summary remark in 13:52 where the disciples are said to be full of joy and the Holy Spirit.

At the crucial council in Jerusalem recorded in Acts 15 we hear Peter remark about Gentiles: "and God, who knows the human heart, testified to them by giving them the Holy Spirit." The Spirit then is seen as the sort of divine seal of approval, indicating to one and all that they are acceptable. As we have already noted, it is also the Holy Spirit who helps make the final ruling about Gentile Christians and their activities (15:28), and who forbids Paul to go into Bithynia (16:7).[21] We may also have a reference to Apollos as boiling over in the Spirit in (18:25), though it is possible that a less literal translation like "with burning enthusiasm" (NRSV) captures the gist of the text at this point.

The discussion between Paul and "some disciples" in Acts 19:1-7 is an intriguing and much disputed one. It appears on the whole that Luke is referring to disciples of John the Baptist, who had not prior to meeting Paul even heard about the Holy Spirit. In other words, they are not Christian disciples who sometime after they accepted Christ were baptized in/by the Spirit. This is why Paul must go through the entire initiation/conversion process with them, first baptizing them and then laying hands on them so that they receive the Holy Spirit. They stand in contrast with Apollos at the end of Acts 18, who knows the way of the Lord, preaches him with zeal, but needs further instruction about Christian baptism.[22]

The famous Miletus speech in Acts 20 includes a reference to the Holy Spirit testifying to Paul in every city that imprisonment and perse-

21. Here for the first and only time called the Spirit of Jesus. This comports with the general pattern of Lukan divine speech in Acts. In general the further the story gets away from Jerusalem, the more specifically Christian and the less specifically non-Christian Jewish the diction becomes. See Ben Witherington III, *The Acts of the Apostles* (Grand Rapids: Eerdmans, 1998), pp. 147-53.

22. See Witherington, *Acts of the Apostles*, pp. 566-72.

cutions await Paul in Jerusalem (v. 23). This presumably alludes to the testimonies of prophets to him about what is yet to come (see, e.g., 21:4).[23] Notice too at 20:28, Paul says that it is the Holy Spirit who has made these Ephesian elders into overseers of the flock in that region. This comports with what we heard in Acts 13 where it was said that Paul and Barnabas were set apart as missionaries by the direction of the Holy Spirit. The Holy Spirit also casts a decisive vote in regard to the Decree in Acts 15. Luke's ecclesiology seems remarkably pneumatic rather than early Catholic. Luke is not even concerned to record what happened to most of the Twelve, or how they related to or influenced their successors. The Agabus warning recorded in Acts 21:11 does not deter Paul either, and it is interesting that the congregation he is with does not simply take the prophecy as an indication that Paul should not go to Jerusalem. Indeed, they say at 21:14 — the Lord's will be done. Perhaps we are to think the Spirit is just warning Paul that things will get difficult for him when he goes to Jerusalem.

It is intriguing that in the chapters about the legal wrangling over Paul, and about the sea voyage, the Holy Spirit is not referred to (no references in Acts 21:12–28:25), not even in the recounting of Paul's conversion in Acts 22 (see vv. 14-16; cf. Acts 9:17-19; 26:19-20). The final reference to the Spirit in Acts comes at 28:25 where we are told that it was the Holy Spirit who spoke to Israel in the Isaianic prophecies, in this case in Is. 6:9-10. This is interesting because here Luke confirms not only the relationship of the Spirit to the inspired text of the Hebrew Scriptures, but stresses that the same Holy Spirit who has been speaking to Christians in the events recounted in this book also spoke to the Jewish ancestors. In other words, the coming of the Spirit on Elizabeth or Mary or the church was not the beginning of the story of the Holy Spirit. The Spirit as a personal being has a history with God's people. The Spirit is not merely a power or a force. It will be well to remember

23. The phraseology is interesting at 21:4 — through the Spirit they told Paul not to go to Jerusalem. This presumably means by means of the Spirit, which in turn would seem to mean when they were in an ecstatic state or being prompted by the Spirit. The odd thing about this is that Paul ignores these warnings of the Spirit, if such they were, believing that God wants him to go to Jerusalem.

this conclusion when we come to the Pauline material and also to John's Gospel, to which we turn next.

III. The Paraclete as Agent and Advocate in the Fourth Gospel

The first reference to the Holy Spirit in John's Gospel comes in the Fourth Evangelist's distinctive recounting of John the Baptist's testimony about Jesus. It is John who says he saw the Spirit descending upon and remaining on Jesus (Jn. 1:32), and we are told that John was informed by God that the one on whom he saw the Spirit descend would be the one to baptize others with the Holy Spirit (1:33). There is a stress in this account on the Spirit remaining on Jesus.

The second reference to the Spirit comes in the famous dialogue with Nicodemus in John 3 where we hear that "no one can enter the Dominion of God without being born of water and of Spirit." The text goes on to say that flesh is born of flesh and Spirit gives birth to spirit. The term "water" here likely has nothing to do with water baptism, but rather is a metaphorical way to refer to physical birth, a birth "out of water" to be contrasted with spiritual birth which is a birth "out of Spirit."[24] Water and Spirit are seen as the mediums or agencies by which such a birth transpires. A person who is born of the Spirit knows where things come from and where they go. That is, he or she knows that this spiritual birth comes from God, just as Jesus comes from God. Jn. 4:24 refers to God being spirit, but this is indeed a discussion about the Father's divine nature, not about the person called the Holy Spirit. Humans must learn to worship with their whole being and in truth, in authentic fashion.[25] Nor is it clear that Jn. 6:63 is about the Holy Spirit. Spirit is opposed to flesh, and the former is said to give life. But is this the spirit of God, or the Holy Spirit which is meant? The second half of

24. See Ben Witherington III, *John's Wisdom* (Louisville: Westminster/John Knox, 1995), pp. 94-97.

25. On this text see pp. 103-5 above.

127

the verse claims that Jesus' words are spirit and life. This supports the conclusion that Jesus is not talking about the Holy Spirit here. The commentary of the Evangelist at Jn. 8:39 indicates that Jesus spoke about the Spirit but only elliptically (in terms of rivers of living water flowing out of a person). More important is the comment that follows, saying that believers were to receive the Spirit but "as yet there was no Spirit because Jesus was not yet glorified." The Synoptic and Johannine Evangelists agree that the Spirit was not dispensed to the disciples prior to the death of Jesus. It rested on Jesus, but not on his disciples during the ministry. They also agree that Jesus offered little or no public teaching on the Spirit during his ministry, apart perhaps from a promise that the Spirit would be coming.[26]

We come now to the discussion of the Spirit in the Farewell Discourses. There are some five Paraclete sayings in John's Gospel, all in the Farewell Discourses (14:26; 15:26; 16:7-11, 12-15). The one Jesus promises to send to the disciples, or have the Father send to them (cf. 14:26 to 15:26), is called a *parakletos* or to be more specific *another parakletos*. There is an implied comparison between Jesus and the Spirit. They are both persons who have the same agendas and function and power. Does the term in question mean Counselor, Comforter, or Advocate? An examination of the passages in the Farewell Discourses about the Spirit suggests the Spirit has a threefold task: (1) to indwell the believer and convey the divine presence and peace, including Jesus' presence, to the believer (14:17-20, 27); (2) to teach and lead the believer into all truth and to testify to the believer about and on behalf of Jesus (14:26 and 15:26); (3) to enable the disciples to testify about Jesus to the world and by means of the Spirit's guidance convict the world about sin, righteousness, and judgment (15:26-27; 16:8-11). The Spirit is clearly seen as Jesus' agent just as Jesus is seen as the agent of the Father on earth (see 16:13-15). It is also true that judicial language is used of the Spirit's role in these discourses, language

---

26. The discourse with Nicodemus is a private one, and at night, just as the discussions about the Spirit in the Farewell Discourses are private discussions with a few disciples.

that favors the translation "Advocate." Jesus is the "Advocate" of the Father and the Spirit is the Advocate of the Son. It is the task of an advocate to speak on behalf of and as a representative of the one who sent him. For our purpose it is crucial to stress that only a personal being can be an Advocate, and the comparison with the Son's role further reinforces the conclusion that the Fourth Evangelist sees the Spirit in personal and divine terms — distinguishable from the Father and the Son, yet working in concert with them as part of the divine identity. The Spirit is Jesus' surrogate on earth when the Son returns to the Father. He will equip the disciples with the presence of Jesus, the understanding of Jesus' teaching, and the power to convict and convert the world, as well as with the perseverance to endure persecution. The ultimate goal of the Spirit is the salvation of the individual through sanctification in the truth, and through such persons the salvation of at least some in the dark world.

This brings us to the final reference to the Spirit in the Fourth Gospel at Jn. 20:22. The risen Jesus breathes on the disciples and says "Receive the Holy Spirit." Is this the Johannine version of Pentecost as some have thought? Such a suggestion seems unlikely, not least because the disciples are no different a week later. They are still frightened and hiding behind locked doors. They are not showing any signs of the effects of the Spirit mentioned in the Farewell Discourses. They do not yet set out on their missionary work. Thus we must see Jesus' act as a prophetic sign promising the Spirit after he returns to the Father (which is what the Farewell Discourses said must happen before the other Advocate could come). Thus the Fourth Gospel agrees with the Synoptics that the Spirit was not given prior to Jesus' departure from this earth. But the Farewell Discourses do enrich our understanding of the Spirit as Jesus' secret agent on earth. What we also find in the Fourth Gospel is very little use of impersonal language to speak about this most personal of beings — the one who dwells within the believer, and who acts for and like the Son.

IV. The Spirit in the Pauline Corpus

The evidence of the Pauline corpus is our earliest window on what was thought about the Holy Spirit at the beginning of church history. It is important to stress at the outset, however, that mention of the Spirit is so frequent in Paul's letters that it is quite impossible to present here all the results of analyzing the more than one hundred occurrences. While Paul only uses the full name "Holy Spirit" some 16-17 times, the terms "his Spirit"/"Spirit of God" some 16 times, and the phrase "Spirit of Christ"/"his Son" three times (Gal. 4:6; Rom. 8:9; Phil. 1:19), he uses the term *pneuma* some 145 times in his letters, and in the vast majority of cases, the Holy Spirit is meant.[27] In contrast to the author of Luke-Acts, Paul never speaks of being "filled with the Holy Spirit."[28] The primary way Paul expresses the initial receiving of the Spirit is either to talk about God giving his Spirit, placing it within you (1 Thess. 4:8; 2 Cor. 1:22; 5:5; Rom. 5:5; Eph. 1:7; 2 Tim. 1:7) or he may talk about the supplying of the Spirit (Gal. 3:5; Phil. 1:19), or he may speak of believers receiving the Spirit (1 Cor. 2:12; 2 Cor. 11:4; Gal. 3:2, 14; Rom. 8:15) or of their simply having the Spirit (1 Cor. 2:16; 7:40; Rom. 8:9).[29] It is interesting that Paul tends to avoid images for the Spirit that imply an impersonal power (e.g., water, oil, wind, fire). We must concentrate in the first instance on Paul's stress on the personal nature of the Holy Spirit.

Many times in the Pauline corpus the term "Spirit" or "Holy Spirit"

---

27. Fee, *God's Empowering Presence*, pp. 14-15.

28. Eph. 5:18-19 may be thought to be an exception to this rule, but it is not. Being drunk with wine is opposed to being full/filled in spirit. The verb is an imperfect passive meaning "let yourself be filled . . ." (ongoing action). The author does not say "become filled." It is not a matter of receiving the Spirit or receiving a second dose of the Spirit, but rather of being filled with the Spirit who already dwells within the believer. The idea is of the Spirit penetrating one's whole being and inspiring one to sing various kinds of songs. Furthermore, the verb *pleroo* with the preposition *en* means "be filled by means of the Spirit," not be "full of the Spirit" as if the Spirit were the content of the filling. When one is fully inspired by the Spirit, one is led to sing songs, and hymns, and spiritual songs. See Ben Witherington III, *Paul's Narrative Thought World* (Louisville: Westminster/John Knox, 1994), p. 285.

29. See Fee, *God's Empowering Presence*, p. 830.

is coupled with verbs that indicate a personal agency is involved. For example, the Spirit cries out from within us (Gal. 4:6), has desires that oppose "the flesh" (Gal. 5:17), leads us in God's ways (Gal. 5:18; Rom. 8:14), and bears witness with our human spirits (Rom. 8:16). The Spirit intercedes for us (Rom. 8:26-27), helps us when we are weak (Rom. 8:26), strengthens believers (Eph. 3:16), and is grieved by human sinfulness (Eph. 4:30). In addition, the Spirit searches all things (1 Cor. 2:10), even searching and knowing God's mind (1 Cor. 2:11). The Spirit dwells among and within believers (1 Cor. 3:16; Rom. 8:11; 2 Tim. 1:14), and the Spirit teaches the gospel to believers (1 Cor. 2:13).

Another clear clue that Paul sees the Spirit as a person is that he will predicate the same activity of the Spirit as he does of Christ or of God. For example, in 1 Cor. 12:6-11 God is said to produce a variety of activities in various people, but notice in v. 11 the Spirit is also said to produce these activities. Or again, in Rom. 8:26 it is said that the Spirit intercedes for the believer, while only a few verses later in 8:34 Christ is said to intercede for believers.[30]

There have been times when scholars have become confused about how Paul views the relationship between the Spirit and Christ, because he will frequently predicate the same thing of both persons. We have life in Christ, but also in the Spirit (cf. Col. 3:4 to Rom. 8:11), joy in Christ, but also in the Spirit (Phil. 4:4 to Rom. 14:17), righteousness from Christ, but also from the Spirit (Phil. 3:8-9 to Rom. 14:17). It is, however, a salient mistake to think that Paul simply identified the Spirit with Christ, or simply saw the Spirit as a non-corporeal manifestation of Christ — Christ's Spirit, so to speak, or the form in which Christ now comes to believers after his glorification. No, Paul knows quite well that Christ is the one who died and rose again, not the Holy Spirit, and he is perfectly capable of distinguishing the two even when referring to the current life of the believer. For example, the Christian is meant to follow the example of the "faithfulness of Jesus Christ" and have faith in Christ, but Paul says nothing of following the example of the "faithfulness of the Spirit." This is because Christ, in a way that is untrue of

---

30. See Fee, *God's Empowering Presence,* pp. 830-31.

the Spirit, was a historical figure who could set such a paradigm for other historical persons to follow.[31] While it is quite true that Paul does reflect on the close working relationship between Christ and the Spirit, especially in the life of the believer, it is simply untrue that he views the Spirit in strictly Christological terms.

Against such a conclusion Gordon Fee rightly points out: (1) that only three times does Paul refer to the Spirit of Christ. Paul primarily concentrates on the Spirit's relationship to the Father. In particular it is the Father who sends the Spirit into believers' lives (Gal. 4:6; 1 Thess. 4:8; 2 Cor. 1:22; 5:5; etc.); (2) the phrase "Spirit of God" or "Spirit of Christ" refers to the activity of God or Christ that is being conveyed to the believer by the Spirit. It is not an indication of some sort of ontological equation of Father or Son with the Spirit. (3) In particular, in the three places where Paul refers to the Spirit of Christ he is referring to the work of Christ in some manner. (4) The point of such phrases as "Spirit of God" or "Spirit of Christ" is to distinguish this Spirit from other sorts of spirits, or to put it the other way around, to identify this Spirit through the Spirit's relationship to the Father or to Christ. Notice how in Rom. 8:9-11 the Spirit of God is absolutely identified with the Spirit of Christ. It is one and the same Spirit. It is just that now the Spirit carries on the work of Christ as well as the work of God. Or again, notice how in 1 Cor. 2:12-16 to have the Spirit of God is the same as having the mind of Christ (or at least the former is the means to the latter). It is true that "Christ and his work give definition to the Spirit and his work in the Christian life";[32] it is not true that Christ and the Spirit are simply equated, even at the level of Christian experience. This brings us to the main text which has tended to cause the misunderstanding that Christ = Spirit in Paul's thought — 2 Cor. 3:17-18.

In the first place 2 Cor. 3:17-18 is alluding to Ex. 34:34. What we have here is an imaginative exegesis or application of an OT text. A

31. For a thoughtful refutation of the views of scholars ranging from A. Deissmann to J. D. G. Dunn on this matter see Fee's *God's Empowering Presence*, especially pp. 831-45.

32. Fee, *God's Empowering Presence*, p. 837, whose lead we are following throughout this portion of this chapter.

proper expansive rendering of the key text goes as follows: "Now the term 'Lord' here (in this text) means the Spirit, and where the Spirit of the Lord is, there is freedom." Notice how the Spirit and the Lord are actually distinguished in the second half of this key text. Two other texts are also, wrongly, thought to suggest a "Spirit Christology" — 1 Cor. 6:17 and 1 Cor. 15:45. The former text is about spiritual union between the believer and Christ. Paul says, "Anyone united to the Lord becomes one spirit with him." The term "spirit" here should not be capitalized, and is not in most recent translations (see, e.g., the NRSV). Paul then is not saying that being united to the Lord can simply be equated with being united to the Spirit without remainder. Indeed, the Spirit does not come up for discussion here at all. There is rather a contrast between the physical union with the prostitute and the spiritual union with Christ.[33] 1 Cor. 15:45 is a more difficult text, for it refers to the last Adam as a life-giving spirit. The context here is a contrast with the first Adam who was a living, breathing human being. Paul is referring to the risen Christ, and what he became as a result of the resurrection. The background to the discussion here is found in vv. 21-22, where Paul has said that all will be made alive through Christ because resurrection has come on the human scene through him and his experience. This is contrasted with how death came through the first Adam. The issue in 1 Cor. 15:45 is soteriological, not Christological. Paul will go on to speak about a spiritual body that can be contrasted with the physical body. Christ is the one who gives life to those who are in him, as the one who already has the resurrection or spiritual body. The parallelism with the first Adam is what has dictated the phrase "life-giving spirit" (as opposed to the living *psuche* that describes the first Adam). "Paul makes a play on this language. The one who will 'breathe' new life into these mortal bodies — with life-giving *pneuma* (as in Ezek. 37:14) and thus make them immortal — is none other than the Risen Christ. . . .

33. Paul could perhaps have said that it is the Spirit which produces such a union between the believer and Christ, but even if this was what he meant he would not be identifying Christ and the Spirit. The Spirit would be the means, and Christ the end or object of the union or relationship. See below on 1 Cor. 12.

The concern . . . therefore, is not christological, as though Christ and the Spirit were somehow now interchangeable terms for Paul. Indeed, he does not intend to say that Christ became *the* life-giving Spirit, but a life-giving spirit."[34]

One further possibility is worth pondering. Sometimes the word "spirit" is used in the NT to simply refer to a supernatural being other than the Holy Spirit, such as an angel or a demon. The term could apparently be used in a generic sense to refer to any sort of supernatural being, even including a divine being such as Christ. We see the generic sort of use of the term *pneuma* in texts like Heb. 1:14 or 1 Pet. 3:19, in the former referring to angels, in the latter to demons or fallen angels. That latter text also stresses that Christ was made alive in the spirit after he died. Once one has passed into the spiritual realm, it appears one could be called a spirit. Perhaps Paul is using the term in this broader more generic way in 1 Cor. 15:45.

Having said all of this it must also be stressed that Paul does indeed believe that the Spirit and Christ have a close relationship with each other and work closely together. For example, in Rom. 8:26-34 Paul says both that Christ intercedes for us, and also that the Spirit does so. But the Spirit does so on earth from within the life of the believer, while Christ is in heaven interceding from there. When Paul uses the language of indwelling he can almost identify the function of Christ and the Spirit. Rom. 8:9-10 refers to our having the Spirit of Christ, while Eph. 3:16-17 actually refers to Christ within the believer. Had Paul worked out the nuances he might have suggested that the Spirit conveys to the believer the very presence of Christ, even though Christ remains in heaven at the right hand of God.[35] "Thus when Paul in Gal. 2:20 . . . speaks of Christ as living in him, he almost certainly means 'Christ lives in me *by his Spirit.*'"[36] Paul will go on to stress immediately after Gal. 2:20-21 that the primary question about the Galatians (as about himself) is whether they had received the Spirit or not (3:2). For

---

34. Fee, *God's Empowering Presence*, pp. 266-67.

35. See Fee, *God's Empowering Presence*, p. 838.

36. Fee, *God's Empowering Presence*, p. 838.

Paul as for Luke, the presence of the Spirit is the sine qua non of the Christian existence. The means of Christian existence is the presence of the Spirit; the end or focus of that existence is Christ and his example.

This last point is made especially clearly in 1 Cor. 12:13. In that text Paul says that by the one Spirit "we were all baptized into one body . . . and we were all made to drink of one Spirit." Notice the stress here on the one Spirit. Paul is making clear that there are not many spirits with which Christians have to deal. It is this one Spirit who joins a person to the body of Christ and provides the spiritual sustenance one needs thereafter to survive as a Christian. It is the one true Spirit of God that also prompts the true confession of Jesus as Lord by the believer (1 Cor. 12:3).[37] There is no such thing as a true Christian without the Holy Spirit in one's life.

Paul is at least functionally Trinitarian in his thinking on these matters. We may illustrate this last point by looking at several key texts. The way a person worships says a lot about a person's faith. In 2 Cor. 13:13 we find a remarkable benediction — "the grace of the Lord Jesus Christ, the love of God, and the communion of the Holy Spirit be with you all." Here we see once more the dramatic effect that the death and resurrection of Jesus and the giving of the Holy Spirit had on a monotheistic Jew's understanding of God.[38] The grace, love, and communion Paul refers to are all gifts of God. Yet each person of the Godhead can be said to make his own contribution to the life of the believer.

In fact, Paul finds it quite natural to speak in a Trinitarian fashion. Notice, for example, how in 1 Cor. 12:4-6 he can refer to a variety of gifts, services, and activities, but one and the same Spirit, one and the same Lord, and one God involved. Or again notice when Paul gives thanks to God in 2 Thess. 2:13-15 he does so because God chose the Thessalonians, the Spirit sanctified them, and they look forward to obtaining the glory of the Lord Jesus Christ. Eph. 4:4-6 of course also comes readily to mind where we hear of one Spirit, one Lord, and one

---

37. Notice how in 1 Cor. 12:3 the Spirit is called both the Spirit of God and the Holy Spirit.

38. See pp. 73-75 above on 1 Cor. 8:6.

God and Father of all. Even if this is by a later Paulinist it is clearly in the spirit of the functional Trinitarianism we find in Paul's earlier letters (cf. 1 Thess. 1:4-5; 1 Cor 2:4-5; Rom. 8:3-4).[39] It is thus fully warranted to conclude not only that Paul sees the Holy Spirit as part of the divine identity but also as much more than just an impersonal force or power. No, the Spirit is a teacher, a sanctifier, a guider, one who has desires for the believer, and one who produces gifts and fruit in the believer. To the activities of the Spirit in the life of the believer we now turn, having carefully demonstrated the personal and divine character of the Spirit in Paul's thinking.[40]

To judge by current discussion in the church, one might assume that Paul focuses his discussion on the gifts of the Spirit almost singularly and only occasionally refers to the fruit of the Spirit (once? — Gal. 5). This conclusion is not really justified, not least because all of Paul's letters are occasional in nature and if the Corinthians had not been struggling with the issue of spiritual gifts and their proper expression we might not even have the discussion we currently find in 1 Cor. 12–14. With occasional letters it is hard to know where the emphasis lies in Paul's thought world. What can be said with some certainty is that in all his letters Paul is concerned with the character of his converts, and the fruit of the Spirit has to do with character traits and their manifestation in Christian living. That Paul believed the way one exercises one's spiritual gifts should be normed by the fruit of the Spirit is shown quite clearly by the fact that he interrupts the discussion of the gifts in 1 Cor. 12–14 to discourse at length on the chief fruit of the Spirit, love, and how love is the manner and means that should dictate how gifts are exercised. We will accordingly consider briefly what Paul says about the fruit of the Spirit.

First, it is quite clear that the Spirit in question in Gal. 5:16-25 is the Holy Spirit. Paul is in the midst of a discussion about the tug of war be-

39. See Fee, *God's Empowering Presence*, pp. 841-42.

40. To a large extent Fee is combating the efforts of various scholars, particularly and most recently Dunn, *Jesus and the Spirit* (Philadelphia: Westminster, 1975), who tend to talk about a Spirit Christology, or all too often reduce the Spirit to an impersonal force or power.

tween the Spirit and the flesh in the life of the believer. The Spirit is trying to pull and guide the believer in the direction of a more Christ-like character. If believers will walk by the Spirit they will not indulge the desires of the flesh, but must continually submit to the guidance of the Spirit. It is a common point but one that needs restressing: Paul does not refer to "fruits" of the Spirit but to "fruit." The implication is that he expects all of these traits to be manifest at one point or another — and in one way or another — in the normal Christian life. Paul is talking about certain character traits that should manifest themselves in interpersonal behavior. Paul discourses on individual aspects of this fruit in numerous places in his letters. For example, at Rom. 5:5 he speaks of the love of God that has been poured into the believer's heart by the Spirit. This reminds us that when Paul is speaking of the fruit of the Spirit he is not talking about natural character traits, but something supernatural produced in the believer that may have little or nothing to do with one's natural inclinations or traits. The discourse on love in 1 Cor. 13 has sometimes been said to involve a character description of Christ (particularly vv. 4-7), and there can be little doubt that Paul sees the Spirit's work as conforming a Christian to the image of Christ.

The joy Paul refers to in Gal. 5 is not a product of circumstances or temporary pleasures but is a result of the internal work of the Spirit within a person (Rom. 14:17). It can even exist in the midst of suffering because it knows that eventually God will fulfill his promises (Rom. 5:2-11). The peace Paul refers to is chiefly peace with God wrought by Christ's death (Col. 3:15), but it also involves peace between believers and between believers and their neighbors as well. It is the polar opposite of a divisive spirit or a spirit of disorder and dissension (Rom. 15:33; 1 Cor. 14:33). Patience involves having a slow fuse, not being quick to anger. It also involves a willingness to bear wrong in love (1 Cor. 13:4).[41] There are of course other traits that Paul refers to but these are sufficient to show that Paul is referring to dispositions that should result in certain kinds of behaviors. Specifically the fruit foster fellowship and

---

41. See the more lengthy discussion in Witherington, *Paul's Narrative Thought World*, pp. 295-300.

concord between believers, thus uniting the body of Christ. By contrast, sin is divisive and produces disorder and chaos in the community. Paul believes that God is already working in the believer by means of the Holy Spirit those virtues that Paul then expects and explains must be worked out in human relationships. If Christians walk in the Spirit they will not merely avoid the indulgences of the flesh, they will model the character of Christ. This is an important point. The Spirit's work points toward Christ, and seeks to shape Christians in Christ's image. We do not hear Paul speaking about focusing on the Spirit or having faith in the Spirit or following the example of the Spirit. The Spirit points away from himself to Christ. The Christian faith is meant to be Christocentric, not pneumatocentric. The Spirit is God and Christ's agent in the believer. Bearing this is mind we turn briefly to a discussion of the gifts of the Spirit in 1 Cor. 12–14.

When Paul talks about the gifts of the Spirit, it is quite clear that he thinks very differently about them than he does about the fruit of the Spirit. About the latter he expects all Christians to manifest all the fruit in one way or another, but as for the gifts he is quite clear that they are parceled out differently to different persons by the Spirit. The rhetorical questions in 1 Cor. 12:29-30 must be taken with absolute seriousness. Each question in the Greek begins with the word "not." The only appropriate response to each question is no. Paul is saying, "Not all speak in tongues, do they?" He then expects no to be the answer to each of these questions. Not all prophesy, not all speak in tongues, not all perform miracles. Thus gifts are distributed throughout the body for the common good. This in turn makes it necessary for Christians to rely on one another if the full complement of gifts is to be exercised in the body.

1 Cor. 12:11 is a crucial verse in this entire discussion. It tells us that all spiritual gifts are allotted and activated by the Holy Spirit, not some other source, and it is the Spirit who chooses which gift to allot to which person. It could hardly be clearer that Paul views the Spirit as a rational being capable of making rational choices. It is also notable that Paul ranks the intelligible gifts highly, specifically gifts of preaching, prophecy, and teaching, ahead of gifts of healing or wonder working or speaking in tongues (12:28-31). In 1 Cor. 14:1 he will urge pursuing the

gift of prophecy. Presumably what he means by this is that one can peti-
tion the Spirit for some particular gift, but the Spirit will decide who
gets what and when. Paul clearly believes that God is a God of order,
and that gifts are given to enhance not detract from order in the body.
Paul does not dismiss the gift of tongues; indeed he says he has and exercises the gift (14:18). But this angelic prayer language, he believes,
should not be spoken in worship unless there is an interpreter to make
it possible for all to benefit from the experience. One gets the impression that the majority of spiritual gifts are speech gifts that aid in the
proclamation of the truth of the gospel in one way or another, though
some gifts also focus on physical injuries and illnesses and in the case of
tongues there is a focus on enhancing the prayer and praise life of the
individual Christian. The communal or more social gifts are stressed. It
is interesting that Paul speaks in 1 Cor. 14:16-17 of the apologetic value
of a gift like prophecy, but in the main the focus of most spiritual gifts
(apart perhaps from the gift of evangelism or preaching) seems to be
the building up of the body of Christ and its internal life.

What we have seen thus far in the NT is the emphasis on both the
personal nature and the activities of the Holy Spirit. It is not possible to
derive a pneumatic Christology from these texts, but it is clear enough
that authors like Luke or Paul or the Fourth Evangelist do wish to stress
how closely the Spirit and Christ or the Spirit and God, or all three,
work together.

V. The Spirit in the General Epistles and Revelation

There are some documents in the NT where the Spirit is hardly mentioned at all. For example, in James and 2 and 3 John there are no references to the Spirit, and in Jude there is just one reference in v. 20 to
praying in the Spirit, which may correlate with what Paul is talking
about in Romans 8 when he speaks of the Spirit crying "*abba,* Father."[42]
There is but one important passage in 1 Peter and one in 2 Peter about

---

42. On which see pp. 29-31 above.

the Holy Spirit, and both have to do with the fact that the Spirit inspires prophetic speech. 2 Pet. 1:20-21 states: "no prophecy of Scripture is a matter of one's own interpretation, because no prophecy came by human will, but men and women moved by the Holy Spirit spoke from God." This text is interesting not least because it suggests that the source of the utterance is God the Father, but the motivator or inspirer who moved the person to speak at all was the Holy Spirit. The author does not believe that there is a significant human contribution, other than men and women being mouthpieces. It is significant that the author mentions both prophets and prophetesses, and we may hear an echo here of Joel 2, and perhaps a memory of the inaugural Christian message given by Peter in Acts 2.

Even more significant is 1 Pet. 1:10-12, which speaks of OT prophets searching about the person and the time God had in mind when there was reference to sufferings and glory destined for the Messiah. What they were told is that they were serving a later generation of believers, not their own generation, with such prophecies. The author of 1 Peter clearly believes in predictive prophecy. He calls the inspirer of such prophecy "the Spirit of Christ within them" (1:11). This phrase likely refers to the same Spirit referred to in v. 12 — the Holy Spirit sent from heaven who spoke the Good News through human emissaries who brought Peter's audience the message. Why then does the author refer to the Holy Spirit as the Spirit of Christ? Is he advocating a pneumatic Christology? While not impossible, a more likely explanation is as follows: (1) the author believes that the same Holy Spirit that inspires Christian speakers in his era also inspired the OT prophets in their day; (2) he believes that since it was Christ who sent the Holy Spirit to believers in this era, the pre-existent Christ may have been responsible for sending the Spirit before to inspire the prophets of old; (3) therefore the "Spirit of Christ" is the Spirit who came from Christ and inspires speech and prophecy about Christ in every era of human history. One further reason for not identifying Christ and Spirit in this text is the fact that the author refers to the sufferings Christ is destined to endure, something he would not wish to predicate of the Spirit.

The book of Hebrews does not have a plethora of references to the

Holy Spirit, but the ones present are significant. In Heb. 2:4 it appears we have something of an intertextual echo of 1 Cor. 12:11. Here, however, we are told that it is God who distributes the gifts of the Holy Spirit, and does so as part of the testimony about the great salvation first declared by the Lord. The implicit Trinitarianism of Heb. 2:3-4 needs to be recognized. Jesus is the Lord (having already been said to be the pre-existent Son in Heb. 1) who first declared eschatological salvation had come, to which God the Father added his testimony by signs and wonders, and by gifts of the Holy Spirit.

The second reference to the Holy Spirit comes at 3:7 where we are told that it is the Holy Spirit who "says" what we find in Ps. 95:7-11. From a Christian perspective the Holy Spirit is the Spirit of prophecy in all ages, even though these early Christians believed the Spirit was not given as a permanent possession prior to the time of Jesus. We see this very same phenomenon at Heb. 10:16-17 where the Spirit is the one speaking, offering the material found in Jer. 31:33-34.

Heb. 6:4 is a crucial text when the issue of perseverance of believers comes up. We are told that a person who has shared in the Holy Spirit but then turns away cannot be restored again to repentance. It is also said of such a person that he or she has been enlightened and has tasted of the heavenly gift and has tasted the goodness of God's word and the powers of the age to come. A more complete description of a Christian person is hard to imagine. For this author as for Paul and others in the NT, having shared in the Holy Spirit is the sine qua non for declaring a person to be a Christian. Notice the author does not say having a share of the Holy Spirit, as if it were a substance that could be parceled out to various people, but literally "having become a participator of the Holy Spirit." One takes part in rather than takes a part of the life in the Spirit.

As is well known, the author of Hebrews engages in quite a lot of typological exegesis of OT texts and institutions. At Heb. 9:8 during the course of explaining about the tabernacle and the priest's role, he refers to the fact that the way into the eternal sanctuary had not yet been disclosed while the first tabernacle was still standing. He adds that it is the Holy Spirit who indicates by the existence of the tabernacle that the ultimate state of affairs had not yet come to pass. This appears to mean that the Holy Spirit was the one who inspired the words of the Scriptures about the instructions for the high priest and for making atonement. The Spirit knew in advance that a greater tabernacle was to come, and by the limitations of the first tabernacle and its continued existence there was an indicator that more was yet to come. The first tabernacle was but an ante-type of the true sanctuary and was less perfect in nature and in effect (only dealing with unintentional sins) than the one which was to come. Here again we see the Christian notion that the third person of the divine identity pre-existed and was active in Israel's history.

At Heb. 10:29 we find the interesting phrase "Spirit of grace." This may be a reference to the Holy Spirit who was being outraged by the rejection of Christ and his atoning death by some. Notice the predication of the personal emotion of "outrage" to the Spirit.

Our last document to consider is of course the last book of the New Testament — Revelation. Here we are imbedded in the world of apocalyptic where there are always some surprises. In terms of basic perspective John seems to vary little from other NT writers. He believes the Holy Spirit is God or Christ's agent or representative on earth, since both the Father and the Son are now in heaven. This is why it is, for instance, that it is both the Spirit and the Bride who bid Christ the bridegroom to return to earth at the close of the book (Rev. 22:17). The Spirit speaks with and through the church, and from the church's perspective.

John, heavily influenced as he is by the OT, finds some creative ways to talk abut the Holy Spirit. As Bauckham has suggested, it appears likely that his use of the seven Spirits of the seven churches image is indebted to Zech. 4:1-14. Indeed, writes Bauckham, "It seems to have been the key Old Testament passage for John's understanding of the role of the Spirit in the divine activity in the world."[43] The vision is intended to teach Zerubbabel that it is by God's Spirit that things will truly be accomplished (4:6). The image chosen is of seven lamps with seven lips

---

43. Bauckham, *The Theology of the Book of Revelation* (Cambridge: Cambridge University Press, 1993), p. 110.

(v. 2), but in a change of the metaphor Zechariah also speaks of the seven eyes of the Lord which range throughout the whole earth. As Bauckham stresses, one of the main questions Revelation seeks to answer for its audiences is how God's plan will be worked out on earth, given the beastly empire and seemingly irresistible evil and power of it. John's answer is the same as Zechariah's — the Spirit of God will accomplish it. But there is more to the vision in Zechariah than is immediately evident on the surface. It is likely that John would have connected the seven lamps with the seven-branched lamp stand that stood in the Temple (see Ex. 25:31-40). Thus it is not a surprise that in John's vision he sees the seven lamps which he identifies as the seven Spirits burning before the throne of God (= the mercy seat of God in the Holy of Holies). But we must remember that the heavenly sanctuary was seen as the model for the earthly one, and in fact Ex. 40:25 speaks directly of the seven lamps that burned before the Lord in the earthly tabernacle.

If we have any doubts that the seven Spirits belong to the divine identity, Rev. 1:4-5 offers us a Trinitarian blessing that includes the seven Spirits before the throne. But the seven Spirits are associated closely not only with God but with Christ, for at Rev. 5:6 the Lamb is said to have seven eyes which are the seven Spirits of God sent out into all the earth (echoing Zech. 4:10b). As Bauckham stresses, the eyes of Yahweh not only indicate God knows all that happens on earth, but also he is able to act powerfully on the basis of this knowledge wherever he chooses. Thus "the seven Spirits are the presence and power of God on earth bringing about God's kingdom by implementing the Lamb's victory throughout the world."[44] But there is more to the seven Spirits than just being a force or a power. John indicates by this bifurcation of the Spirit that each of his seven churches has full measure of the Holy Spirit; none are shortchanged in terms of the power or presence or revelation

---

44. R. Bauckham, *God Crucified: Monotheism and Christology in the New Testament* (Grand Rapids: Eerdmans, 1998), p. 113. I would disagree, however, with his further conclusion that the Spirit is then seen as the divine power which is now the Spirit of Christ or the manner of Christ's presence on earth. It seems clear to me that in fact the Spirit is seen as a person distinguishable from Christ, as the final presentation of the Spirit and the Bride speaking in Rev. 22:17 suggests.

of God. And as elsewhere in the NT where we have seen the Spirit having a role of intercession for believers,[45] so here the seven Spirits represent the Spirit interceding before the throne of God on behalf of these persecuted churches. Only persons, not forces, can so intercede.[46] But the Spirit not only represents the church to God, it also represents Christ to the church, serving as Christ's agent as Rev. 5:6 suggests.

Apart from the discussion of the seven Spirits, there are fourteen references to the Holy Spirit in Revelation; all of them have to do with the Spirit being the source of John's prophecy. Without question the dominant image of the Spirit in this book is as the Spirit of prophecy, which is no surprise considering how very Jewish this work is. It is perhaps possible to make a distinction between the seven Spirits which say something about the Spirit's mission to the world (see 5:6), and the other references to the Holy Spirit which focus on the activity of the Spirit within and addressing the church.[47] In just one of these fourteen references, Rev. 19:10, there is actually some question about whether the Holy Spirit is meant. There an angel upbraids John for trying to worship him and concludes by saying that the testimony to Jesus is "the spirit of prophecy." It is not clear to me that this is anything other than a metaphorical use of the term *pneuma* meaning something like the essence or focus or gist of prophecy.

Four of the other thirteen references refer to the actual moment of inspiration when John received a vision through the Spirit. Thus in Rev. 1:10 and 4:2 we hear that he was "in the Spirit," and two other times we hear that the angel carried him away by means of the Spirit (17:3; 21:10; cf. Ezek. 3:12-14). The way this is described suggests an ecstatic and overpowering experience of some sort that had a visionary component. As Bauckham notes, these four references are strategically placed so as

---

45. See pp. 29-32 above.

46. It is also well to keep in mind that the generic term "spirit" whether referring to Christ or some other supernatural being such as an angel or demon (see pp. 103-5 above) refers in such cases to a personal entity, not a mere force or power. This is true here in Rev. 1 as well.

47. See D. Hill, "Prophecy and Prophets in the Revelation of St. John," *New Testament Studies* 18 (1971-72): 401-18.

to make clear that the whole of John's visionary experiences came through the agency of the Holy Spirit. But Bauckham appears also to be correct that the "Spirit does not give the content of the revelation, but the visionary experience which enables John to receive the revelation."[48] The revelation comes from God or Christ but by means of the agency of the Spirit. As we have seen in 22:17 the Spirit is able to speak for himself, and we see another example of this in Rev. 14:13. John is quite capable of distinguishing the Spirit from Christ, and it would be a mistake to see the Spirit as simply the mouthpiece of either God or Christ. The Spirit is seen as a distinguishable personal entity, working on earth in close consort with God and Christ in heaven.

The book of Revelation provides yet one more example of how Old Testamental images and ideas affected early Christian portrayal of the Spirit. This did not, however, prevent them from emphasizing in various ways the personal nature of the divine Spirit, nor did it prevent them from making appropriate distinctions between the Spirit and Christ or God. The book of Revelation is in some ways the most explicitly Trinitarian of all NT books, and it shows where the discussion of the Spirit could and would be furthered in the post-canonical period.

VI. Conclusions

As we approached the third person of the Trinity our task was to go beyond the Old Testament understanding of the Holy Spirit and embrace the New Testament understanding in which the Holy Spirit becomes not just a power or force but a person distinguishable from both the Father and the Son. Many of the Old Testament beliefs included the theology that God's presence equaled God's spirit and that circumstances seemed to determine the random distribution of God's spirit. In essence, as witnessed through the prophets and prophecy, God's spirit could be given and/or withdrawn at any given time without regard to a person's faith-

---

48. Bauckham, *God Crucified*, p. 116. Here and throughout this section we are indebted to Bauckham's penetrating insights.

fulness or sinfulness. The spirit of the Old Testament provided guidance and revelation through prophecy but was not found to be a separate entity. This theology contrasts the understanding represented in the New Testament, in which the Holy Spirit is not only spoken of in personal terms but is clearly a separate person from the Son of Man.

Jesus himself gives witness to the Holy Spirit in the Synoptics and in John. Matthew and Luke provide evidence that clearly distinguishes the Holy Spirit as an animate force (since one cannot blaspheme an inanimate object) and thus brings the third person into the Trinity paralleling the Son of Man. The Fourth Gospel adds to this picture the pre-Easter promise of the Holy Spirit which will be given to believers after Jesus' death. The Holy Spirit is said to lead, guide, promote, and drive but not dominate, in contrast to the unclean spirits Jesus encounters during his ministry. And it is not until after the death and resurrection in Matthew 28:19 that the Holy Spirit is included in the divine name — the singular noun indicating the one God who has a tri-personal nature. But, it is still apparent that the Gospels do not give as clear a picture of the Holy Spirit as the book of Acts.

It is in the book of Acts where the Spirit is seen as the primary agent of action. Acts 1:8 emphasizes the Spirit as the personal agent who will supply the disciples and believers with power. Earlier we had noted that the disciples' power to cast out demons and to heal came through the name of Jesus and/or their association to him, but after the death of Jesus the Holy Spirit comes into full play; it is this Holy Spirit who empowers the disciples and believers to work miracles. In Acts 2:33 Jesus receives the "promise of the Holy Spirit," and it is this Spirit which he pours out upon the disciples. The three — the Father, the Son, and the Holy Spirit — are in heaven together. They are all part of the divine identity as the sending of the Spirit is passed from Father to Son so that God's people will be equipped to spread the gospel. The Spirit's coming is associated with new and refreshing life. As it is in the Old Testament, the coming of the Spirit is associated with the coming of the presence of God, but it is even more.

This is a presence which once it is received is kept and not withdrawn, and as our evidence shows it is a presence that comes only with the acceptance of Jesus Christ, not by water and not by actions.

Furthermore, the Pauline corpus supports the personal agency set forth in the Gospels and Acts. Although Paul does not speak of being filled with the Spirit, he does speak of God giving or supplying of his Spirit or of believers receiving the Spirit. As we noted, it would be a mistake to misunderstand the words of the apostle and identify the Spirit with Christ or the limited Old Testament understanding. Rather, it is quite clear that Paul knows that Christ is the one who died and rose again, and it is the Holy Spirit who comes as the comforter and helper.

The benediction found in 2 Cor. 13:13 lends further support by addressing all three persons of the Godhead. Each person, the Father, Son, and Holy Spirit, has his own contribution to bring to the believer's life — grace, love, and communion. It is Paul who provides the believer with the fullest picture of the Holy Spirit yet. The Spirit is a teacher, a sanctifier, a guider, one who produces gifts and fruit within the believer. The Spirit brings order and unites the believer to the body of Christ.

The General Epistles and Revelation continue to support our findings throughout the New Testament. There is a clear distinction between the spirit or presence of God in the Old Testament and the third person of the Trinity known by believers in intimate terms as the Holy Spirit. It can truly be said that the Old Testament images and ideas had an effect on how new believers understood the Son of Man and the Holy Spirit. They were separate persons within the divine identity, each with a specific purpose and place. The monotheistic God was understood more fully as the definition was expanded to include the Son of Man and the Holy Spirit.

QUESTIONS

1. In the OT the Holy Spirit is understood to be the spirit of God and although divine, not necessarily separate from God. This understanding is said to be different in the NT.

   A. Discuss the significance of the NT understanding that the Holy Spirit is the third person of the divine identity, separate in personhood yet the same in essence or nature.

B. Give evidence to dispute the theory that the Holy Spirit is the spirit of the risen Christ or merely the spirit of God.

2. It is noted throughout the chapter that the Gospel of John contains more references to the Holy Spirit than the Synoptic Gospels. Consider the audience, purpose, date, and focus of the Fourth Gospel and discuss your own ideas as to why the author provides more insight into the Holy Spirit, especially in the pre-Easter discourses.

3. In the OT the Holy Spirit is understood to be the spirit of God which moves and works in people at various times and especially through prophetic experiences. The prophets are "overcome" by the spirit for a defined period of time. This seems contradictory to the experiences witnessed in Acts in which the Spirit is poured out upon a believer and remains with that person unless he/she falls from faith.

   A. Considering the discussion given by the authors, how do the life, death, and resurrection of Christ influence and determine this change?

   B. How does your answer support or refute the statement that "one can no more have a little bit of the Spirit than one can be a little pregnant" (implying that one receives the full amount of the Spirit at the time of belief)?

4. It is suggested by C. K. Barrett that one of the reasons for the paucity of the references to the Holy Spirit in the Synoptics (and especially on the lips of Jesus) is the secrecy of the messiahship of Jesus. Many prophets in the OT manifested the Holy Spirit but were not mistaken for the Messiah.

   A. How was Jesus different than a prophet? Why was it important that Jesus not be mistaken as merely a prophet?

   B. What would have happened if Jesus had poured out the Spirit upon the disciples while he was still with them?

Scripture Index